There She Grows

WOMEN IN PLANT NAMES

There She Grows

WOMEN IN PLANT NAMES

BRENDA LEESE

Brenda Leese

Pixel Tweaks Publications
SELF-PUBLISHING MADE SIMPLE

Published in 2018 by Brenda Leese

Flora **Features**

© Copyright Brenda Leese

Illustrations © Sophie Holme
www.sophieholme.co.uk

ISBN: 978-1-9998936-1-3

Book Design by Russell Holden
www.pixeltweakspublications.com

Pixel Tweaks Publications
SELF-PUBLISHING MADE SIMPLE

Printed by Ingram

FOR MARY

PREFACE

My interest in plants started at a very young age. My earliest recollection is of regularly walking home from primary school alongside a disused, water-filled gravel pit and noticing, to me, some very unusual and striking plants growing on the water's edge. They were unlike the other plants and shrubs along the gravel pit. What were they? I had to find out. They were horsetails (*Equisetum*) – and I was hooked!

My favourite subject at school was biology and I went on to London University and a degree in botany and biochemistry, followed by a DPhil from the University of York in plant biochemistry.

Despite the move into biochemistry, I had always been interested in taxonomy or classification and perhaps should have been a librarian or worked in a museum where I could follow these up more closely.

So where did the idea for this book begin? I was aware that books about plant hunters rarely featured women, and that male plant hunters often had plants named after them. What about those plants named after women? Why was it that their lives rarely featured in any books about plant discoveries? Perhaps there was no story to tell? It was not until much later when I enrolled for a BTec in horticulture that the opportunity arose to test the feasibility of writing this book. A project was required and mine looked into the idea of writing about the lives of women who had plants named after them. I found that there were many plants named after women but that their life stories were less likely to be written about in this context than the lives of men. This book, therefore, focuses on the biographies of women who have had plants named after them. It provides some information about the plants – their botanical and common names, family and country of origin - but does not give details about how to grow them. Such information can be found elsewhere.

I decided early on to focus on genus and species names rather than cultivars. Cultivar names are used in horticulture and as a botanist by background I wanted to concentrate on plants that were found in the wild. The naming of plants is complex and still evolving, so for the women in this book to have been immortalised in a plant name or names is quite an achievement and they deserve to be more widely known. The writing of this book is a small step in that direction.

The book begins with an introduction about life at the time that these women were living. The chapters are then arranged chronologically with Chapter 2 covering women of the 17th and 18th centuries, Chapter 3 the 19th century and Chapter 4 the 20th century. Chapter 5 digresses a little and describes three women whose plants are associated with the US state of Oregon. Chapter 6 covers the women about whom I could find very little information, in particular their dates so they could not be included in earlier chapters. The final chapter summarises the findings and the characteristics of this remarkable group of women.

Brenda Leese 2018

CONTENTS

Chapter 4
The Twentieth Century

Chapter 5
The Oregon Connection

Chapter 6
The Ones That (Almost) Got Away

Chapter 7

CHAPTER
•ONE•

INTRODUCTION

This is a book about the lives of women who have had one or more plants named after them in the form of a genus or species. It is not a book about the plants themselves, although some details are given. Women who have had cultivars named after them are not included in the book since such names are specific only to horticulture. Some of the women included here feature in other books, for example, on botanical artists. These include Marianne North, well-known for her gallery at Kew Gardens, and Maria Sibylla Merian whose work was the subject of an exhibition at The Queen's Gallery in London in 2016. There is a book concerned with cultivar names and the people behind those names[1] but no others, as far as I am aware, feature women with genera or species named after them. This book aims to correct that omission.

The Beginning

The initial problem was where to begin. Although books about male plant hunters are relatively common, those featuring women are less so.[2-5] What would be the best way of identifying plants named after women? Out of several books that list the derivation of plant names, I decided to select the one by Coombes[6] which lists plants alphabetically by genus and the species associated with the genus, as well as the origin of the names. For those named after people, male names are listed by their initial and surname and female names by their full first name and surname so making it easy to identify the women. After identifying the female names they were grouped together in terms of similarities. Where possible I have used original sources of information about their lives. For each woman in the book, some basic information is provided about the plant named after her: specifically its botanical name, common name (if any), plant family and country of origin. Where the woman has more than one plant named after her, one has been selected for the profile and the others listed in the text. If possible, a picture of the plant and of the woman after whom it is named has been included, followed by details of the person's life. In some cases no picture of the woman has been found.

This method of selection has provided many women's names but lacks any indication of what proportion of women giving their names to plants are represented. It feels rather like being on the edge of a pit and not knowing how deep it is. Coombs only states that his book provides '..*names of the more commonly grown plants,*' but further details have not been forthcoming.[6] There are approximately 352,000 species of angiosperms (flowering plants), approximately 16,000 genera and 620 families.[7] However, these numbers are approximations since new species are constantly being added and names are frequently changed. Furthermore, there is an online list of 175 cacti named after women, plus a further similarly sized list of succulents.[8] The women profiled in this book therefore represent a small sample of those recognised in plant names but their biographies nevertheless provide an interesting insight into their lives.

Summary of Findings

The women identified from Coombes can be divided into four distinct groups.[6] The first group comprises women who were themselves plant hunters and went on expeditions overseas, who went to live overseas or who went plant hunting near where they were living. They were plant hunters themselves or botanical artists, botanists or horticulturalists, and sometimes more than one of these. For simplicity, and a lack of any other suitable definition I have designated this group as 'Plantswomen' in the broadest use of the term: to mean women who know about plants. Many of the women in this group had no formal botanical or horticultural training yet were able to create a significant niche for themselves. The second group consists of the wives (and some other relatives) of male plant hunters, with plants named after them by their husbands. The third group comprises royalty or other members of the aristocracy and the fourth group, goddesses in mythology. With the last named group it became clear that the word 'female' should be used rather than 'women' because the goddesses cannot be regarded as 'women.' The numbers in the four groups are as follows:

Plantswomen..n=31
Wives...n=21
Royalty and Aristocracy..n=9
Mythological Females..n=14
Total...n=75

At this point a decision was made to confine this first book to the group of Plantswomen. The second book will be about the wives, the royalty and the goddesses. Thirty-one women were identified from Coombes [6] who were themselves Plantswomen and for whom one or more plants have been named. During the course of researching their lives, an additional three women were identified and included. This means that this book recounts the lives of 34 women after whom plants have been named.

The women are represented in 26 different plant families, the largest of which, with four representatives each, are the Orchidaceae (Orchids) and the Iridaceae (Irises). Table 1.1 sets out the plant families and the women associated with those families. It should be noted that some of the 34 women had more than one plant named after them. In these cases one plant was selected as representative of the women and details included. Other plants named after these women are mentioned in the text but not illustrated or included in Table 1.1.

Table 1.1

Plant Families & the Women Named after Plants in those Families

PLANT FAMILY	NAME	NUMBER
Acanthaceae	Fittons	2
Aizoaceae	Bolus	1
Amaryllidaceae	Clive	1
Apocyanaceae	Beaumont	1
Aquifoliaceae	Meserve	1
Asparagaceae	de Brimeur	1
Asphodelaceae	North	1
Asteraceae	Milford	1
Bromeliaceae	Mee	1
Convolvulaceae	Berry	1
Crassulaceae	Daigremont	1
Ericaceae	Davis; Leach	2
Euphorbiaceae	Robb	1
Fabaceae	Northampton	1
Gesneriaceae	Smith	1
Hyacinthaceae	Saunders	1
Iridaceae	Libert; Mason; Merian; Danford	4
Malvaceae	Burgess	1
Nyctaginaceae	Butt	1
Oleaceae	von Josika	1
Orchidaceae	Moss; Tankerville; Lawrence; Harrison	4
Plantaginaceae	Barrett	1
Plumbaginaceae	Willmott	1
Rosaceae	Fedchenko	1
Scrophulariaceae	Barber	1
Vitaceae	Coignet	1
Total		**34**

These women collected plants from every continent. Of the 33 species or genera represented, eight (24%) originate from South Africa, 5 (15%) from South America, four (12%) from Europe, three (9%) from the USA, and three from Asia. The others are from Australia, China, Brazil, West Indies, Madagascar, Mexico, Japan, New Zealand, Tanzania and one worldwide. (Table 1.2)

Table 1.2
Country / Region of Origin of Plants Named after the Women

ORIGIN	NAME	NUMBER
Asia	Beaumont; Fedchenko; Tankerville	3
Australia	Northampton	1
Brazil	Mee	1
China	Willmott	1
Europe	de Brimeur; Danford; Robb; von Josika	4
Japan	Coignet	1
Madagascar	Daigremont	1
Mexico	Smith	1
New Zealand	Libert	1
South Africa	Barber; Bolus; Clive; Mason; Merian; Millford; North; Saunders	8
South America	Lawrence; Butt; Fittons; Harrison; Moss	6
Tanzania	Burgess	1
USA	Barrett; Davis; Leach	3
West Indies	Berry	1
Worldwide	Meserve	1
Total		**34**

In total, 18 (53%) of the women are British with four (12%) from the USA, and two each are from France, Belgium and Ireland (Table 1.3). Other countries with one representative are Germany, Hungary, Jamaica, Russia, South Africa and Trinidad.

Table 1.3
Country of Birth of the Women

COUNTRY OF BIRTH	NAME	NUMBER
Belgium	Libert; de Brimeur	2
France	Coignet; Daigremont	2
Germany	Merian	1
Hungary	von Josika	1
Ireland	Fittons	2
Jamaica	Berry	1
Russia	Fedchenko	1
South Africa	Bolus	1
Trinidad	Butt	1
UK	Barber; Beaumont; Burgess; Clive; Danford; Harrison; Lawrence; Mason; Mee; Milford; Moss; North; Northampton; Robb; Saunders; Smith; Tankerville; Willmott;	18
USA	Barrett; Davis; Leach; Meserve	4
Total		**34**

The ways in which these women developed their interest in plants ranged from 27 (79%) who were noted horticulturalists, enthusiasts or collectors, 13 (38%) who were botanists, 8 (24%) who were botanical artists, and one about whom nothing is known (Table 1.4). It is interesting to note that 14 (41%) of the women developed connections with either Kew or the botanical gardens and research organisations in their own country in order to assist with identification of their plants or for whom they drew their flower pictures (Table 1.4).

Table 1.4

Botanists, Horticulturalists, Collectors and Artists: Who was who?

Name	Botanists	Horticulturalists	Collectors	Artists	Links to famous botanists/institutions
Barber	✓		✓	✓	✓
Barrett	✓		✓		✓
Beaumont		✓			
Berry				✓	
Bolus	✓				✓
Burgess		✓		·	✓
Butt		✓			
Clive		✓			✓
Coignet		✓			
Danford			✓		
Davis	✓		✓		
de Brimeur	✓	✓			
Daigremont	✓				
Fedchenko	✓		✓		✓
Fitton, S	✓				
Fitton, E	✓				
Harrison		✓		✓	✓
Josika, von	✓				
Lawrence		✓			✓
Leach	✓		✓		
Libert	✓		✓		
Mee			✓	✓	✓
Merian			✓	✓	
Mason			✓		
Meserve		✓			
Milford		✓	✓		
Moss		✓			✓
North			✓	✓	✓
Northampton					
Robb	✓		✓		✓
Saunders			✓	✓	✓
Tankerville		✓			
Smith				✓	✓
Willmott		✓			
Total = 34	**13 (38%)**	**13 (38%)**	**14 (41%)**	**8 (24%)**	**14 (41%)**

Around three quarters of the women were of aristocratic background or came from affluent families, enabling them to travel or indulge in their love of plants. Interestingly, it has not been possible to identify the birth and death dates for five of the women and for another two (the Fitton sisters) their dates are estimates, perhaps an indication of how, being women, they have been overlooked historically. A further difficulty is that in some cases their first names have also been impossible to identify, which has added to the problem of finding dates. Some are known only as, for example, Mrs R.V. Butt, Miss Burgess and Mme Coignet. Others are known by their husband's name: for example Elizabeth Harrison is generally referred to as Mrs Arnold Harrison, again perhaps a result of convention in the age in which they living. Table 1.5 shows that most of the women were born in the 18th and 19th centuries at the time when exploration and plant hunting were at their peak.

Table 1.5
Century of Birth of the Women in the Book

CENTURY OF BIRTH	NAME	NUMBER
17th	de Brimeur; Merian	2
18th	Beaumont; Berry; Clive; Fitton,E; Fitton,S; Harrison; Libert; Moss; Northampton; Tankerville; von Josika	11
19th	Barber; Barrett; Bolus; Burgess; Butt; Coignet; Danford; Davis; Daigremont; Fedchenko; Lawrence; Leach; Mason; Milford; North; Robb; Saunders; Smith; Willmott	19
20th	Mee; Meserve	2
Total		**34**

Historical Background

The women featured in this book had plants named after them because they were either plant hunters, botanists, horticulturalists or botanical artists, or a combination of these. What then was the botanical environment in which these women achieved the accolade of having a plant named after them, so perpetuating their name forever?

Plant Hunting

The late 18th and 19th centuries were times of great exploration with the expansion of the British Empire when many exotic plants were brought back to Britain for the first time.[3] Kew Gardens, established in 1759, became prominent as the foremost botanic garden in the world.[9] Until then, plant hunting had been the preserve of private individuals, associations and academic societies but now botanic gardens, and later commercial nurseries (e.g. Veitch) began to sponsor plant hunters in order to increase their stock of exotic plants.[9] Botanic gardens were set up throughout the British Empire, including Calcutta (1787), Sydney (1816) and Colombo (1821).

Britain was not alone; France, for example, was equally interested in botanical exploration. The Jardin du Roi was established in Paris between 1626 and 1640, later being known as the Jardin des Plantes, which received plants from the French colonies, with the Empress Josephine an enthusiast.[9] In the early 19th century in England, botanic gardens were set up in cities and towns such as Liverpool (1836), Sheffield (1836), Birmingham (1832) and Chiswick (1821)[5]. By the 1840s Kew began to publish colonial flora.[9]

Innovations in Plant Transportation

Two innovations in particular made great contributions to the safe transportation of plants, namely the Wardian Case and steamships.

The Wardian Case

Setting out on expeditions to collect plants was all very well, but voyages were long and hazardous and plants had to be kept alive for many months. Dried specimens (herbaria) were fine for identification and classification purposes but not for growing and propagation. Even seeds were problematic and had to be kept dry whereas living plants require moisture.[3] Some innovations helped, notably the Wardian Case, which provided a means of transporting living specimens which could be planted and propagated on return to Britain and was a major innovation that accelerated plant introductions in the 19th century.[5,9,10] The Wardian Case was the idea of Dr Nathaniel Bagshaw Ward who, in 1829, invented a portable, almost sealed glass mini-greenhouse [5,10] in which plants were found to survive lengthy sea voyages.[11] The Wardian Case was tested during an eight month voyage from Sydney to England with the plants arriving in good health.[3] They were placed on a leaf-mould base inside the glass case, where transpiration helped to maintain a moist atmosphere, allowing the plants to thrive.[9] The concept seems obvious today but was novel at that time. Before the Wardian Case cargoes of plants required careful attention to shield them from salt water spray and ship captains could be reluctant to release men for such minor activities, particularly in heavy seas.[3]

Steamships

The introduction of steam speeded up transport considerably and released ships from the vagaries of the weather that beset sailing ships. Voyages were still lengthy, however. Initially steamships retained their sails, but eventually they replaced long-distance sailing ships. The first regular transatlantic service, starting in 1837, was the wooden paddle-steamer SS Great Western, built by Isambard

The SS Great Western

Kingdom Brunel. However, before 1866, steamships were unable to carry enough coal to make voyages to the Far East, or similar distances and have enough space left to carry a commercial cargo, or indeed, plants[12] This meant that, in effect, the major plant hunting sea expeditions used sailing ships.

The Industrial Revolution

The industrial revolution in Britain in the 19th century was also responsible for a growing middle class which had not been established in earlier centuries. These wealthy industrialists had the means to build stovehouses or greenhouses at their mansions which enabled the new tropical plants to thrive in an otherwise hostile climate. Such developments were assisted by the invention of the means to heat the stovehouses by the circulation hot water, but these innovations were the preserve of the rich. Another helpful change was the repeal of the glass tax in 1846. With these developments tropical plants, orchids in particular, became so popular, that the term Orchidomania[9] was used to describe the passion of collectors for these plants.[13] Orchids had been known in China and Japan but it was not until the early 1800s that they were sought by Europeans with Kew beginning their cultivation from 1786.[13,14] Three women in this volume have orchids named after them and were the owners of stovehouses.

The expansion of the British Empire required men to take up positions of governance overseas and many took their families with them. This provided the opportunity for some women to acquaint themselves with the flora of their new surroundings and many became experts, sending their finds back to the UK for identification and naming. Before that, women were either members of a powerful, affluent upper class, living on large country estates with time on their hands, or of the working classes who were poor and lived by farming or by serving the wealthy. Certain activities, including needlework, reading, painting – and botanising – were regarded as suitable for upper class women, and many became experts in plant identification and drawing.[15, 16] It cannot be denied, however, that men were seen as the plant hunters and the few women involved tended to be ignored, with the notable exception of Marianne North.[2] Hyams, in his book of England's Flora, automatically assumes plant hunting to be the preserve of the male. By contrast Short[5], actually apologises for there being just one woman in his study of 38 plant hunters, who was the wife of one of the men in the book. He comments *'The absence of women is primarily due to the fact that the social constraints of the time did not permit women to travel widely, at least not by themselves.'* Short goes on to say *'Furthermore married women, often with large families to care for, had limited opportunities even to step out into the local bush and spend time collecting.'*[5] However, in this book I show that many women did travel alone and made contributions to botanical knowledge.

The Naming of Plants

One question that many ask about the plant hunters is, how did they know the plants they found on their expeditions had not been named earlier? The most likely answer is that they didn't. However, many were experts in plant identification, perhaps of specific families or genera, and took with them any books that were available to them.[17] Nevertheless, plants were sometimes named more than once, which is why some plants were renamed when the duplication became known.[3] Frequently, plant hunters would send their finds to Kew, or other botanic gardens, for verification and authentication of their names. Indeed, it is notable how many women in this book sent copious samples to the local botanic garden or to Kew and frequently became well acquainted with the botanists there. As has been discussed, transporting plant specimens long distances, often by ship was problematic. Dried specimens were the norm but on arrival after a long sea voyage they may not have been in the best condition, causing further confusion in identification.[18,19] It was not until the invention of the Wardian Case in the 1830s that live plant transportation became possible.

The situation became so difficult that rules for the naming of plants had to be introduced. Carl Linnaeus (1707-78), in his volume *Species Plantarum* [20] published in 1753, is credited with the introduction of the binomial system of plant classification consisting of a genus name followed by a species name.[21] This resolved the earlier practice of giving plants lengthy and unwieldy names based on their description. It also solved the problem of different local names for the same plant, and names in different languages – it had to be Latin.[5] Karl Linnaeus was born in Southern Sweden but spent most of his life at Uppsala University where he was professor of botany and medicine. He is the most famous of all Swedish scientists[22] and his life and achievements have been much written about. [23,24,25 25]

Following on from Linnaeus's classification, the International Code of Botanical Nomenclature was adopted at a congress in Vienna in 1905, and adjusted at six-yearly intervals as required.[26] This was followed by the International Code of

The Linnaeus Garden, Uppsala

Nomenclature for Cultivated Plants founded in 1953, which again proceeded through a number of revisions and included the names of garden and cultivated plants.[27] One important aspect of these rules is that of the *'application of the principle of priority.* [28] The first name given to a plant that has been published has absolute priority, which provides another reason for the female plant hunters to send their specimens to a botanic garden. However, more recently, developments in genetics have caused some plants to be reclassified. The naming of plants is more complex than might be imagined and is still evolving, so for these women to be immortalised in a plant name is quite an achievement and they deserve to be more widely known. This book is a small step in that direction.

Photography

Photography as we know it can be said to have began in the late 1830s in France where Daguerrotypes were the forerunners of modern film. In the 1870s dry photographic plates became available and cameras could be hand held rather than static. However, it was not until the 1880s when rolls of film were invented by George Eastman that cameras and photography became more popular and widely available, though film was still expensive.[29] For the women in this book who lived in the eighteenth and early nineteenth centuries this meant that only those from affluent families had the means to have their portraits painted. It was not until much later that photographs became available. For some women in this book, portraits or photographs are therefore not available.

The Role of Women

As we have seen, during the 18th and 19th centuries, the role of women was generally confined to the home so enabling men to go on plant hunting expeditions overseas and make names for themselves. Such restrictions did not, however, extend to botanical drawing and painting which were regarded as suitable pastimes for wealthy women. Kramer[30] heads one of his chapters *'a genteel diversion,'* aptly summing up male views of these talented women and there are numerous examples of women who did make contributions but were criticised or ignored for their efforts, by men. For example, Lemmon's book, published in 1968[11] sets out to *'pay tribute to the backroom men of flora* (my under-lining)... *to tell only the stories of these men most of them unchronicled, unhonoured and unsung.'* These *'backroom men'* include Francis Masson, David Douglas and Sir Joseph Banks, amongst others! Hardly obscure? However, Kramer[10] tells the life stories of some 30 female botanical artists of the 18th and 19th centuries. He notes the large number of women illustrators producing botanical works of art that went largely unrecognised and even denigrated because of their gender, regardless of their artistic merit. Many women published anonymously because they knew that if they used their own name their work would be ignored or dismissed as unworthy.[31] Although women such as Matilda Smith were contributing drawings and paintings to botanical magazines and books, Kramer found that details of their lives remained obscure, a problem encountered in writing this book about women.[31,32] Wilfrid Blunt, the art historian, was particularly negative about women's contributions and failed to acknowledge them.[33] He was especially critical of Marianne North as *'lacking in sensitivity,'* and of Matilda Smith, he commented, that she should be remembered for her *'untiring efforts rather than her skills.'* [30,32] Would he have said the same of a man? Despite these problems women were quietly and enthusiastically pursuing their botanical art.

Of course, women were not helped in the botanical world by being excluded from learned and scientific societies.[31] John Lindley in particular wanted botany to be a serious scientific subject for men and not an amusement *'for ladies'* who were regarded as *'amateurs.'* Since women were, in any case, excluded (by men) from the scientific community it is surprising that any succeeded, but they did. Amusingly, Horwood[31] recounts that Mrs Henrietta Moriarty's paintings were dismissed as *'too good to be done by the hand of a women;'* and, on a rare occasion *'Robert Backhouse assisted his wife in developing daffodils'–* though Mrs Backhouse's first name is not recorded! This book is an attempt to bring these women's lives and achievements to a wider audience.

References

1. Pankhurst, A. *Who does your Garden Grow?* Earl's Eye Publishing, Colchester, 1992.

2. Hyams, E. *The Story of England's Flora.* Kestrel Books, England, 1979.

3. Campbell-Culver, M. *The Origin of Plants.* Random House, London, 2001.

4. Gribbin, M. & Gribbin, J. *Flower Hunters.* Oxford University Press, Oxford, 2008.

5. Short, P. *In Pursuit of Plants.* Timber Press, Cambridge, 2004.

6. Coombes, A. J. *A-Z of Plant Names.* Chancellor Press, London, 1994.

7. *The Plant List. Version 1.1*, www.theplantlist.org, 2013.

8. Wiktorowski, K. *Women and Cacti.* www.kwiki.republika.pl/wom.html

9. Aitkin, R. *Botanical Riches: Stories of Botanical Exploration.* Lund Humphries, London, 2008.

10. Hepper, F.N. *Plant Hunting for Kew.* HMSO, London, 1989.

11. Lemmon, K. *The Golden Age of Plant Hunters.* Phoenix House, London, 1968.

12. MacGregor, D.R. *The Tea Clippers, their History and Development 1833-1875.* Conway Maritime Press, London, 1983.

13. Kramer, J. *A Passion for Orchids.* Prestel, London, 2002

14. Fry, C. *The Plant Hunters.* Carlton Books Ltd. London, 2012.

15. De Bray, L. *The Art of Botanical Illustration.* Quarto Publishing, London, 1989.

16. Seaton, V. *The Language of Flowers.* University of Virginia Press, 1995.

17. Gibbons, W. *How do you know you have found a new species?* archive-srel.uga.edu/outreach/ecoview070121.htm, 21 January, 2007.

18. Brittain, J. *Plants, People and Places.* Outhouse Publishing, Winchester, 2005.

19. Jeffrey, C.J. *An Introduction to Plant Taxonomy.* Cambridge University Press, 1982.

20. Linnaeus, K. *Species Plantarum.* Sweden, 1753.

21. Natural History Museum. *Carl Linnaeus.* www.nhm.ac.uk/nature-online/science-online.html

22. Broberg, G. *Carl Linnaeus.* Swedish Institute, Copenhagen, 2006.

23. Buchan,U. & Colborn, N. *The Classic Horticulturalist.* Cassell, London, 1987.

24. Morton A.G. *History of Botanical Science.* Academic Press, London, 1981.

25. Pavord, A. *The Naming of Names.* Bloomsbury, London, 2005.

26. McNeill, J. et al. *International Code of Botanical Nomenclature.* www.iapt-taxon.org/nomen/main.php, 2011.

27. Brickell, C.D. et al. *International Code of Nomenclature for Cultivated Plants.* 9th edition, ISHS, Leuven, June 2016.

28. Stearns, W.T. *Dictionary of Plant Names for Gardeners.* Timber Press, Cambridge, 1972.

29. Hirsch, R. *Seizing the Light: a History of Photography.* McGraw-Hill, New York, 2000.

30. Kramer, J. *Women of Flowers.* Welcome Books, New York, 1996.

31. Horwood, C. *Gardening Women.* Virago, London, 2010.

32. Penn, H. *An Englishwoman's Garden.* BBC Books, London, 1993.

33. Blunt, W. *Art of Botanical Illustration.* Dover Publications, New York, 1950.

CHAPTER
· TWO ·

THE SEVENTEENTH & EIGHTEENTH CENTURIES

Maria Sibylla Merian (1647-1717)

Emma Tankerville (1752-1836)

Diana Beaumont (1765-1831)

Maria, Lady Northampton (1766-1843)

Anne Marie Libert (1782-1865)

Dorothy Hall Berry (1784-1846)

Charlotte Clive (1787-1866)

Hannah Moss (1787-1872)

Elizabeth Harrison (1792-1834)

Sarah Fitton (1796-1874)

Rosalia von Josika (1799-1850)

Elizabeth Fitton (1817-1866)

The Seventeenth Century

Maria Sibylla Merian is one of the best known of the women in this book and the only one to have been born in the 17th century. At that time women were expected to stay at home and certainly not to travel as she did, making her achievements even more exceptional. Moreover, at this time, plant hunters and travellers did not receive any sponsorship or finance and had to fund everything from their own resources.[1] Maria financed her travels by selling her paintings, which included images of insects as well as plants, for both of which she is now justly famous.

The Eighteenth Century

A feature of the eleven women in this chapter born in the 18th century, is, in most cases, their affluent backgrounds which enabled them to pursue their interests unhindered by the need to earn a living.

Of the eleven women, Elizabeth Fitton was actually born in the 19th century but is included here since she worked with her older sister, Sarah. Seven of the women were from England and five grew plants in their stove- or green-houses at their residences (Emma Tankerville, Diana Beaumont, Charlotte Clive, Hannah Moss and Elizabeth Harrison). It is notable that the four women who were botanists (the Fitton sisters, Rosalia von Josika and Anne Marie Libert) were not English (the Fitton sisters being from Ireland) and that five English women (notably Emma Tankerville, Diana Beaumont, Charlotte Clive, Hannah Moss and Elizabeth Harrison) are best described as horticulturalists with their stove-houses of exotic plants and some with links to Kew. By the late 18th century when these women were collecting, exotic plants were being brought in from the British Empire as well as from other European countries with empires, such as France and The Netherlands.[1] However, although botanical art was considered to be a suitable activity for a woman, it is notable that only two of the women (Dorothy Berry and Elizabeth Harrison) were artists.[2]

The interest in exotic plants and their influx from all parts of the world lead to Liverpool becoming an important port for the arrival of many of these plants after long voyages. It is therefore not surprising that three of the women in this book who were active around this time lived in or near Liverpool. Hannah Moss (1787-1872) and Elizabeth Harrison (1792-1834) were both residents of Liverpool and collectors of orchids whilst Dorothy Hall Berry (1784-1846) also lived there. Miss Burgess (see Chapter 6), of whom little is known, lived in nearby Birkenhead before moving to South Africa. She is linked with John Medley Wood, an Englishman who lived in a house called Otterspool in South Africa the same name as Hannah Moss's house in Liverpool. Furthermore, a Richard Harrison (possibly Elizabeth Harrison's brother-in-law) is mentioned in connection with railway development in Liverpool alongside John Moss, Hannah Moss's husband.[3] These are intriguing connections and it is interesting to speculate that they all knew each other or at least some members of their respective families. Biographies of each of the twelve women follow, in chronological order.

Maria Sibylla Merian (1647-1717)

Maria Sibylla Merian is an example of an intrepid woman who pursued her interests in natural history despite the traditions of the time when women were generally expected to stay at home.[4]

She was born in Frankfurt into a well-known publishing family. Her Dutch mother, Johanna Sibylla, was the second wife of her Swiss father, Matthias, who died when she was three. Her step-father Jacob Marrel, a Dutch painter, taught her how to paint flowers, at which she showed exceptional talent.[5] However, her real interest was in the metamorphosis of insects, starting with silkworms.[5] She published a book on the life cycle of butterflies, particularly the caterpillar stage, which helped make them known to the general public at a time when the true nature of metamorphosis was little understood.[6] Such interests were not really approved of as suitable for a woman in the 17th century, but she was not deterred.

She had married one of her artist teachers, Johann Graff, in 1665 when she was 18, but the marriage did not last. After leaving her husband in 1685 and retaining her maiden name, she moved from Nuremberg to Holland, first to Friesland into a religious community, and eventually to Amsterdam. She earned a living from embroidery and painting portraits to support her two daughters, Johanna Helena and Dorothea Maria.

In 1699, at the age of 52, she moved to the Dutch colony of Surinam in South America with her daughters, travelling and sketching local animals and plants, discovering many that were previously un-catalogued.[2] Maria preferred to paint from living rather than dead specimens. However, she was forced to return to Holland after two years when she became ill, but continued drawing until having a stroke in 1715, dying two years later. Many of Maria's paintings are characterised by the depiction of both plants and insects in accurate detail.

She published her work as books of paintings and is particularly known for drawing insects on the plants with which they are associated in the wild. Her rarest books are the three volumes of European insects and flowers, published separately in 1675, 1677 and 1680, and in 1680 as the three volumes in one book, the *Neues Blumenbuch*.[7] The images in these books were intended to be used as patterns for embroidery or for artists. In 1705 her *Metamorphosis Insectorum Surinamensium* was published with 60 plates, and was much admired.[6] However, in common with many women of her time, and despite having published important work for which she was acclaimed, it was only after her death when her daughter, Dorothea, published a collection of her work as *Erucarum*

BOTANICAL NAME
Watsonia meriana
COMMON NAME
Bulbil Bugle Lily
FAMILY
Iridaceae
NATIVE OF
South Africa

Ortus Alimentum et Paradoxa Metamorphosis, that she became more widely known.[8]

In all she had seventeen species of plants and animals named after her. The plant chosen here, *Watsonia meriana,* is a herbaceous perennial of the lily family, showing some similarities to *Crocosmia* spp.

More recently Maria's work has been rediscovered and recognised.[9] For example, in Germany in 1987 Maria's portrait was printed on the 500 DM note and on a 0.40 DM stamp. More recently, in 2016 an exhibition of her work at The Queen's Gallery, London, entitled *Maria Merian's Butterflies,* featured paintings collected by King George III, and focused on insects painted with the plants on which they are most frequently found.[5] The pictures are part watercolours and part prints on vellum.

Lady Emma Tankerville (1752-1836)

Emma, Lady Tankerville, came from a wealthy background and was well-known as a collector of exotic plants which she cultivated at her home, Mount Felix, near Walton on Thames, England.[10] She was born Lady Emma Colebrooke, the daughter of Mary Skynner and Sir James Colebrooke, 1st Baronet, who died at the age of 39 years.

Emma married Lord Charles Bennet, 4th Earl of Tankerville in 1771. He was a shell collector and cricket enthusiast and, as such, was a key member of a committee which formulated the 'Leg Before Wicket' rule.[11]

Portrait of Emma, with her daughters Caroline & Anna

The Tankerville fortune came from land in Northumberland at their northern seat of Chillingham Castle. As well as his agricultural wealth the earl's fortune was further enhanced by lead mining near Tankerville in Shropshire, which started in 1830 and was later described as *'....unquestionably one of the greatest, if not the greatest, lead producing lodes in Shropshire.'* This fortune enabled the 5th Earl (Emma's son) to demolish the existing house at Mount Felix and build a new mansion on the same site. Emma's collection of over 680 plant illustrations was purchased by Kew in 1932.

She is commemorated in the orchid *Phaius tankervilleae* (also known as *Limodorum tankervilleae*) which was brought from China by John Fothergill, a doctor and botanist who was also a shell collector and after whom the genus *Fothergilla* is named.

31

BOTANICAL NAME
Phaius tankervilleae
COMMON NAME
Nun or Swamp Orchid
FAMILY
Orchidaceae
NATIVE OF
South East Asia

The plant was later named by Joseph Banks in honour of Emma, in whose greenhouse at Mount Felix it was encouraged to flower.[10] The family's horticultural interests were continued with Emma's daughter, Lady Mary Elizabeth Bennet (1785-1861) who with the help of William Richardson, the gardener at her father's estate, cultivated new varieties of tri-coloured pansies. Lady Mary was also an artist whose pictures are exhibited widely and who lived at Belsay Castle, Northumberland, after her marriage to Sir Charles Miles Lambert Monck.

Diana Beaumont (1765- 1831)

In 1720 an earlier woman named Diana, Diana Blackett (1703-1742), the daughter of Sir William Blackett, who had estates in Northumberland from his fortune in the lead mining industry,[12,13] married Sir William Wentworth and moved to Bretton Hall,[14] near Wakefield, England now the site of the Yorkshire Sculpture Park.

The Wentworths were Yorkshire landed gentry, and had owned Bretton Hall for over three hundred years. They also held land in Surrey where Wentworth Golf Club is now located and in New Hampshire, USA, known as Bretton Woods, where the International Monetary Fund (IMF) was established after the Second World War. Diana Blackett was wealthy and her fortune enabled Sir William Wentworth to improve the Bretton Hall estate. On Sir William Wentworth's death in 1763, the estate passed to his son, Sir Thomas Wentworth who used some of this inheritance to extend and improve the estate further. Even more inheritance came in 1777 when Sir Walter Blackett, an MP and distant relative, died without an heir and left his vast estates in Northumberland to Sir Thomas Wentworth who changed his name to Sir Thomas Wentworth Blackett. Diana Beaumont, an illegitimate daughter of Sir Thomas Wentworth Blackett who remained unmarried, inherited the Bretton Hall estate on his death in 1792. Diana and her husband, Thomas Richard Beaumont, considerably expanded the house.[15]

In 1827, Diana commissioned a domed conservatory measuring 100 feet wide by 60 feet high, which was filled with exotic plants and is said to have been the prototype for the Crystal Palace in London.[16] Sadly it was removed soon after Diana's death. Diana had a rather unfortunate demeanour and was often referred to as 'Madame Beaumont' by her staff, amongst whom she was not particularly popular.

The genus *Beaumontia* was named in her honour. She was described in the *Curtis's Botanical Magazine* in 1833 as *'an ardent lover and munificent patroness of Horticulture.'* *Beaumontia* was described by Dr. Nathaniel Wallich in 1824 from specimens sent to him from Bretton Hall. Wallich was Danish, became the Superintendent of the Calcutta Botanic Garden and was a well-known botanist in India. *Beaumontia grandiflora* had previously been named *Echites grandiflora* from plants found in the forests of Eastern Bengal (India) but its name had not been published legitimately and so Wallich's name is the correct one. This vine-like plant is also known as Herald's Trumpet and Nepal Trumpet Flower.

BOTANICAL NAME
Beaumontia grandiflora
COMMON NAME
Easter Lily Vine
FAMILY
Apocynaceae (Dogbanes)
NATIVE OF
South East Asia

Maria, Lady Northampton (1766-1843)

Maria Smith, daughter of Joshua Smith and Sarah Gilbert of Erle Stoke Park, Wiltshire, England married Charles Compton 1st Marquess of Northampton in 1787.[17]

Joshua Smith was the MP for Devizes in Wiltshire, England from 1784-1796. He built Erle Stoke House between 1786 and 1791, but the house was partially demolished after a fire in 1950 and the grounds are now the site of HM Prison Erlestoke.[18]

Maria's husband, Charles Compton was MP for Northampton from 1784 to 1796. They had two children. His cousin was Spencer Perceval, Prime Minister from 1809 until his assassination in the House of Commons in 1812. Why the Australian lilac vine is named after Maria is unclear.

BOTANICAL NAME
Hardenbergia comptoniana
COMMON NAME
Australian Lilac Vine
FAMILY
Fabaceae
NATIVE OF
Australia

Anne-Marie Libert (1782-1865)

Anne-Marie Libert (also known as Marie-Anne) was another botanist and plant hunter who, despite having no formal training, became a renowned expert on cryptogams, particularly lichens, in her native Belgium and around the world.

She was born in Malmedy, near Liege, the twelfth of 13 children of a tannery owner, Henri-Joseph Libert and his wife Marie-Jeanne-Bernadine Dubois. The family was well-enough off to send Anne-Marie to boarding school from the age of 12 to learn German and violin, in both of which she excelled.[19] Anne-Marie was interested in plants from an early age and took to plant hunting in the area around her home. As well as becoming an important botanist, she continued to support the family tannery business after her parents' deaths with the help of her sister and four of her brothers, none of whom married.

Her collection of plants was used by the well-known Belgian botanist Alexandre Lejeune for his book, *Flora des environs de spa.*[20] Included in this volume were new species discovered by Anne-Marie: *Rubus arduennensis, Rubus montanus, Rosa nemorosa,* and *Rosa umbellata.*

She also collected cryptogams with the Swiss botanist Auguste-Pyrame de Candolle, a professor at Montpellier University, and identified new species.[21] She corresponded with botanists in France,

Germany and Britain about the plants she had named and about her book *Plantae cryptogamicae quas in Arduenna collegit* on which her reputation was largely based.[22]

When she was 55 she decided to stop plant hunting, took up archaeology and continued to be active in local affairs. Anne-Marie's reputation extended well beyond Belgium and she received a number of awards which reflected her courage and determination as well as her success. These included: Associate Libre of the Paris Linnaean Society (1820), a gold medal of merit and a gift of jewels from Emperor Friedrich-Willhelm III, and the presidency of the Natural Sciences section of a scientific congress in Liege in 1836. In addition, she became the first woman honorary member of the Belgian Royal Botanical Society when it was founded in 1862, and was later made a full member.

BOTANICAL NAME
Libertia grandiflora
COMMON NAME
New Zealand Iris
FAMILY
Iridaceae
NATIVE OF
New Zealand

Even after her death in 1865, her reputation continued to grow. Her herbarium was purchased by the Botanic Garden in Brussels. A number of plants were named after her, the genus *Libertia*, named by Lejeune, being profiled here. *Libertia* is a genus of the Iris family which is native to South America, Australia, New Guinea and New Zealand.

Dorothy Hall Berry (1784-1846)

Dorothy Hall Berry was born in Jamaica to Thomas Berry and Dorothy Hall. In 1803 she married Charles Horsfall (1776 – 1846) in Liverpool, England and they had 13 children. Charles was Lord Mayor of Liverpool from 1832–1833.[23] He was an enthusiastic botanist, partly due to his trade with West Africa, the West Indies and the Americas. He also worked in partnership with his cousins, the Hodgsons, who were Jamaican plantation owners.

BOTANICAL NAME
Ipomoea horsfalliae
COMMON NAME
Lady Doorly's Morning Glory
Cardinal Creeper
FAMILY
Convolvulaceae
NATIVE OF
West Indies

Dorothy Horsfall was a noted horticultural artist which accounts for her having a plant named after her.[1] She drew six plates for *Curtis's Botanical Magazine* and contributed to other botanical publications and magazines.[23,24] One of Dorothy's children, Thomas Berry Horsfall, was conservative MP for Liverpool and became mayor, following his father.

Little more is known about her and no picture has been found.

Lady Charlotte Florentia Clive (1787-1866)

The plant *Cliva* was named after Lady Charlotte Florentia Clive, eldest daughter of Edward Clive, 1st Earl of Powis, and granddaughter of the English soldier and colonial administrator Robert Clive (known as Clive of India). She married Hugh Percy, 3rd Duke of Northumberland, in 1817 and became Duchess of Northumberland.[25] They had no children.

She was a keen horticulturalist who was the first to cultivate *Clivia* plants in Europe in her gardens at Alnwick Castle, England. Charlotte's garden at Syon House just outside London has a large conservatory for exotic plants. The house was built in 1830 by her husband, is still lived in by the Dukes of Northumberland and was restored in 2000. Charlotte was appointed governess to Princess Victoria, who became Queen Victoria in 1837.

BOTANICAL NAME
Clivia miniata
COMMON NAME
Winter Lily
FAMILY
Amaryllidaceae
NATIVE OF
South Africa

The 3rd Duke of Northumberland, Charlotte's husband, died at Alnwick in 1847, aged 51. Charlotte, Duchess of Northumberland died in 1866, aged 78 and is buried in the family vault in Westminster Abbey.

William Burchell was an explorer and naturalist who, in 1815, discovered what was to be named *Clivia*, in the forests of the Eastern Cape of South Africa. The Kew botanist James Lindley had also sent James Bowie, a Kew gardener and collector, to the same area, where more plants were collected in 1820. Lindley named the plant *Clivia nobilis* in 1828 at the same time as William Hooker named it *Imatophyllum aitonii*. However, it was Lindley's name that stuck. Lindley stated:

> *'We have named this genus in compliment to her grace, the Duchess of Northumberland, to whom we are greatly indebted for an opportunity of publishing it. Such a compliment has long been due to the noble family of Clive, and we are proud in having the honour of being the first to pay it.'* [25]

Hannah Moss (1787-1872)

Cattleya mossiae was imported into England from Venezuela in 1836 by a friend of a Liverpudlian, George Green, who gave it to Mrs Moss of Otterspool in Liverpool because she had a stove, or greenhouse housing exotic plants in her garden.[26] It thrived and flowered and Mrs Moss was so happy that she sketched it and sent it with the flowers to Sir William Jackson Hooker of the University of Glasgow and later Director of Kew. He recognised it as a new species and named it after Mrs Moss, who was reported to be thrilled.[27]

BOTANICAL NAME
Cattleya mossiae
COMMON NAME
Mrs Moss's Cattleya
Easter Orchid
FAMILY
Orchidaceae
NATIVE OF
Venezuela

So who was Mrs Moss, as she is always referred to? Her first name is not given in any of the letters and publications relating to this plant and her date of birth is equally elusive.[28,29] It is known that she was an orchid enthusiast who lived in Liverpool at a house named Otterspool.[3] In 1811, the newly built house had been acquired by John Moss who owned a timber business and had interests in railways and sugar plantations in Demerara, Guyana as well as owning a bank. He was also a slave owner. Hannah Moss was the wife of John Moss whom she married in 1805 when she was 18 years old and he was 23.

Cattleya mossiae

Hannah was born Hannah Taylor, the daughter of Thomas Taylor of Blakely in Lancashire. She and John had nine children, five of whom predeceased her. Her eldest son, Sir Thomas, was created a baronet in 1868 and took the name Thomas Edwards-Moss after his marriage to Amy Charlotte Edwards in 1847. The dates and correspondence associated with *Cattleya mossiae* all point to Hannah being 'Mrs Moss'. At least one other report assumed that she was Thomas Edwards-Moss's wife Amy, who also lived at Otterspool after John Moss's death, though the dates do not coincide.[30]

In 1843 a *Garden Memorandum* in the *Gardener's Chronicle* [31] noted that there was a large *Cattleya mossiae* plant in the stove house at Otterspool; the original from which Mrs Moss had made her sketch for *Curtis's Botanical Magazine* in 1839.[27,29] *Cattleya mossiae* is the national flower of Venezuela which is close to Guyana where the sugar plantations of John Moss were located.

A picture of Hannah Moss has not been found.

Elizabeth Harrison (1792-1834)

Information about Mrs Arnold Harrison, as she is generally known, is available from a number of early sources,[32-39] but nowhere is she referred to by her own first name, nor are her dates given. It is known that she lived in the early part of the 19th century in Aigburth, Liverpool with her husband, Arnold Harrison, both of whom were avid collectors of orchids. Arnold had three brothers, William, Henry and Richard. William and Henry were cotton merchants who lived in Rio de Janeiro and ran a company known as Messrs. Harrison & Co.[33] They collected orchids from the Brazilian mountains which they sent back to Richard in Liverpool.

One of these was *Biphrenaria harrisoniae* which was described in 1825, as *Dendrobium harrisoniae* in honour of Mrs. Harrison. In 1825 it was transferred to the genus *Bifrenaria*.[34] Later, in April 1833, an unknown species of orchid from the mountains of Brazil which flowered in Mrs Harrison's greenhouse was possibly thought to be *Bifrenaria harrisoniae* or *Cattleya harrisoniana*.[35] A short time later, Mrs. Harrison, who was an engraver,[36,37] sent a drawing and cutting of this plant to the botanist John Lindley, who confirmed it was not only a new species but

BOTANICAL NAME
Biphrenaria harrisoniae
COMMON NAME
Harrison's Biphrenaria
FAMILY
Orchidaceae
NATIVE OF
South America

a new genus. In its description, dated the same year, Lindley suggested the name of *Leptotes*, from the Greek for mild, delicate, in reference to the appearance of the plant's flowers.[37,38] William Harrison also discovered what became known as Mrs Arnold Harrison's Oncidium (*Oncidium harrisonanum*) about which John Lindley noted:

> *'We have taken the liberty of naming it after a family more distinguished that any other for the number of species they have introduced, and for the success with which they have cultivated them. Whenever horticulture shall again find an historian, he will have to record the period when the difficulty of cultivating tropical Orchidaceae, which was once considered insuperable was successfully overcome, in such a history the names of Mr William Harrison, Mr Henry Harrison, Mrs Arnold Harrison and Mr Richard Harrison will stand among the foremost'.*[39]

Another publication of the time indicated that Mrs Harrison had died in 1834 and her orchid collection had been purchased by Mr Knight whose own collection was already renowned.[40] This publication notes that Mr Knight was able to purchase the collection *'because the relatives of this amiable lady had found her favourite plants but a painful, ever present remembrance of their bereavement and so resolved to remove them from their sight.'* It appears the Richard Harrison retained his collection. He was known as *'the leader'* and was *'visited by botanists and men of science from all parts of the world'.*[41] Aigburth had become a *'sort of Mecca, to which the faithful orchid growers made an annual pilgrimage.'*[41]

Mrs Harrison's own collection contained some 160 named and known orchid species, several of which had not yet flowered in England.[40]

Despite these accolades, Mrs Harrison is still known only by her husband's name in all the publications of the time. However, in the preparation of this book, and using a genealogy website, her name, Elizabeth, and her dates have been uncovered, and she can be known by her own name.[42] These findings make clear why there was so much regret on Elizabeth's death at the age of only 43 years, leaving five children aged between 1 and 15 years of age.

There is no picture of Elizabeth Harrison.

Sarah Fitton (1796-1874)
Elizabeth Fitton (1817-1866)

In 1865 Eugène Coemans, a Belgian botanist and Catholic priest identified and named the genus *Fittonia* in honour of two Irish sisters: Sarah
(1796- 1874) and Elizabeth Fitton (1817-1866). Little is known about
the sisters and even their birth dates are estimates. There are no pictures
of them. Sarah Fitton is known for writing *Conversations on Botany'*
(dated 1817):- '*a dialogue between a mother and her little son Edward
about flower and plant structure, as well as plant classification according
to the system devised by Linnaeus.*'[43,44]
The book has 18 chapters and begins:

Edward: '*What are you doing Mamma?*'
Mother: '*I am examining a pretty little yellow flower that we found
this morning in the hedge.*'
Edward: '*How do you examine a flower?*'
Mother: '*You cannot understand the method, my dear, until you
have learned something of botany.*'
Edward: '*What is botany?*'

BOTANICAL NAME
Fittonia albivenis
'Verschaffeltii'
COMMON NAME
Nerve Plant
FAMILY
Acanthaceae
NATIVE OF
Peruvian rainforests

It continues in a similar vein detailing the structure, classification and naming of plants.[45] Elizabeth contributed to later editions of the book, which is available in its entirety online and is a charming read. Sarah lived in Paris for many years and wrote other children's stories. She was clearly well known, being described by Elizabeth Barrett Browning as *'Shrewd kind and rich.'* Sarah dedicated one of her books, *The Four Seasons* to her *'excellent old friend'* Sir William Hooker, Director of The Royal Botanic Gardens, Kew. More is known about Sarah and Elizabeth's brother, William Henry Fitton, who was a geologist and physician.

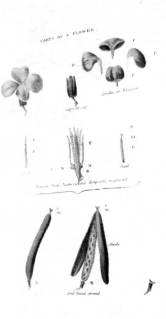

In England, *Fittonia* plants are usually grown indoors for their attractive veined, evergreen foliage. They are regarded as difficult houseplants because of their requirement for high and constant humidity as befits a plant of the tropical rainforests of South America.

There are no pictures of Sarah or Elizabeth.

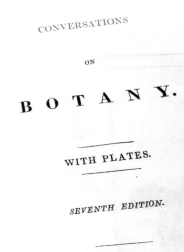

CONVERSATIONS

ON

B O T A N Y.

WITH PLATES.

SEVENTH EDITION.

LONDON:

Rosalia von Josika (1799-1850)

Rosalia was a botanist in what is now Hungary. She found the lilac named after her, *Syringa josikea*, in Transylvania, and realised it was different from the lilacs already known.

BOTANICAL NAME
Syringa josikaea
COMMON NAME
Hungarian Lilac
FAMILY
Oleaceae
NATIVE OF
Central and Eastern
Europe

The plant was found in 1826 and named after her in 1830.[46] Princess Rosalia was one of four children of Count Janos and Theresia Jekelalussy Margitfalva, members of central European aristocracy. She married Baron Johann Josika von Branyicska and became a baroness.[47] Josika Castle in Surduc, Romania, was the home of the Josika family who could have been relatives of Rosalia and her husband.

Information about Rosalia is sparse and a portrait has not been found.

References

1. Aitken, R. *Botanical Riches: Stories of Botanical Exploration.* Melbourne University Publishing, Singapore, 2007.

2. Kramer, J. *Women of Flowers.* Welcome Books, New York, 2005.

3. Trust, G. *John Moss of Otterspool.* Author House UK Ltd., Milton Keynes, 2011.

4. Davis, N.Z. *Women on the Margins.* Harvard University Press, London, 1995.

5. Heard, K. *Maria Merian's Butterflies.* Royal Collection Trust, London, 2016.

6. Merian, M. S. *Metamorphosis Insectorum Surinamensium,* Frankfurt,1705.

7. Merian, M. S. *Neues Blumenbuch,* Johann Andreas Graff, Nuremburg, 1680.

8. Merian, M. S. (1647-1717) & Merian, D.M.H. (1678-1745). *Erucarum Ortus, Alimentum et Paradoxa Metamorphosis.* Johannes Oosterwijk, Amsterdam, 1718.

9. Merian, M.S. *New Book of Flowers.* Prestel, London, 1999.

10. Kilpatrick, J. *Gifts from the Garden of China.* Frances Lincoln, London, 2007.

11. Pall Mall: *The Star and Garter',* Survey of London: 30:1, 351–352, 1960.

12. *The Blacketts of North East England.* www.theblacketts.com.

13. *Dukesfield Smelters and Carriers Project.* www.dukesfield.org.uk.

14. www.bretton-hall.com/archive/time-line.

15. www.rotherhamweb.co.uk/geneology/wentworth.

16. Woudstra, J. *Marnock, Robert and the creation of the Sheffield Botanical and Horticultural Gardens.* Garden History 35(1), 2-36, 2007.

17. www.thepeerage.com.

18. Pevsner, N. & Cherry, B. *The Buildings of England, Wiltshire.* Penguin, UK, 1999, p.241.

19. Creese, M.R.S. *Ladies in the Laboratory. 2 Western European Women in Science 1800-1900.* Scarecrow Press, 2004.

20. Lejeune, A.L. *Flora des Environs de Spa.* 1811.

21. www.america.pink/marie-anne-libert. *Marie-Anne Libert.*

22. Libert, M-A. *Plantae Cryptogamae quas in Arduenna Collegit.* 1830-37.

23. www.ucl.ac.uk/lbs/address/view/1274296544

24. Curtis's Botanical Magazine, 1831-36.

25. Szilard, P. *Clivias (Kaffir Lilies)*. www.tropicalplantsociety.org .

26. Chadwick, A.E. & Chadwick, A.E. *The Classic Cattleyas*. Timber Press, 2006.

27. Curtis's Botanical Magazine RT.3722, 1839.

28. Graham Trust, information from gravestone, personal communication, 2016.

29. Royal Botanic Gardens, Kew. *Letters from Charles S Parker to Sir William Jackson Hooker: c. 1838: re: naming of C.mossiae. 1838.*

30. Kramer, J. A *Passion for Orchids*. Prestel, London, 2002.

31. Moss, J. *Garden Memoranda*. Gardener's Chronicle, vol.3, p.432, 1843.

32. *The History of Orchids.*, Botanical Register. p.41, 1833.

33. Gardner, G. T*ravels in the Interior of Brazil principally through the Northern Provinces and the Gold and Diamond Districts,* London, 1849.

34. Bechtel, H., Cribb, P. & Launert, P. *The Manual of Cultivated Orchid Species*. MIT Press, Cambridge, Mass,. 1986.

35. Orchid Review, 1, 1893.

36. *Harrison, Mrs A. Oncidium auricula orchid.* Sydenham Edwards *The Botanical Register,* London, Ridgeway, 1833.

37. Sims, J. Curtis's Botanical Magazine, 56, 2927, London 1829.

38. Lindley, J. *Leptotes bicolour.* Edward's Botanical Register 19, t.1625. James Ridgway & Sons Ed. London, 1833.

39. Lindley, J. *Oncidium harrisonarum.* Mrs Arnold Harrison's Oncidium. The Literary Gazette, 18, 343, 1834.

40. Gardeners' Magazine vol X, p280, 1834.

41. Gardeners' Chronicle vol.3, p. 838, 1843.

42. *Geni* www.geni.com.

43. George, S. *Epistolary Change:* J. Lit. & Sci. 4, 12-29, 2011.

44. Dictionary of National Biography. Oxford University Press. www.global.oup.com.

45. Fitton, E. *Conversations on Botany*. Longman, Rees, Orme, Brown and Green, London, 7th edition, 1817.

46. *The Lelacke or Pipe Tree.* Arnoldia. www.arnoldia.arboretum.harvard.edu p.114.

47. www.ancestry.co.uk.

CHAPTER
•THREE•

THE NINETEENTH CENTURY.

Louisa Lawrence (1803-1855)

Mary Barber (1818-1899)

Katherine Saunders (1824-1901)

Mary Ann Robb (1829-1912)

Marianne North (1830-1890)

Olga Fedchenko (1845-1921)

Marianne Harriet Mason (1845-1932)

Antoinette Emily Danford (1851-1927)

Matilda Smith (1854-1926)

Ellen Ann Willmott (1858-1934)

Louisa Bolus (1877-1970)

Helen Milford (1877-1940)

In many ways the nineteenth century was similar to the seventeenth and eighteenth in that plant hunting and the discovery of plants new to Europe continued and men achieved the most acclaim.[1] Women, however, continued to cultivate plants, identify them and paint them. Of the twelve women in this chapter only three did not live into the twentieth century; all except two (Olga Fedchenko and Louisa Bolus) were British and all were well enough off to pursue their botanical interests without the need to earn a living. The two non-British women, Olga Fedchenko who was Russian and Louisa Bolus who was South African are best described as botanists, as are two of the British women, Mary Barber and Mary Ann Robb. Just three were horticulturalists: Louisa Lawrence, Ellen Willmott and Helen Milford, the first two of whom had large estates where they cultivated exotic plants. It is notable that of the twelve women, eight were plant collectors overcoming considerable odds in their pursuit of new plants. Three (Mary Barber, Katherine Saunders and Helen Milford) collected in South Africa and Marianne Mason elsewhere in Africa. Mary Ann Robb and Antoinette Danford collected in Europe and Turkey, respectively, whilst the only non-British woman of the eight (Olga Fedchenko) collected in Turkestan. By far the best known of the eight plant collectors is Marianne North, with her gallery at Kew, who collected and painted throughout the world. Links to the important botanic gardens of the day, especially Kew, were important to these women in helping with descriptions and identification of their plants. No fewer than six women corresponded with Kew (Louisa Lawrence, Mary Barber, Katherine Saunders, Mary Ann Robb, Marianne North and Matilda Smith) with the two non-British women, Olga Fedchenko and Louisa Bolus, in contact with St. Petersburg and Cape Town botanic gardens, respectively. Four of the women were botanical artists; Mary Barber, Katherine Saunders, Marianne North and Matilda Smith, all producing botanical drawings for Kew.[2] Biographies of each of the twelve women follow, in chronological order.

Louisa Lawrence (1803-1855)

Louisa Lawrence was a well-known horticulturalist and connoisseur of orchids.
Her mother was Elizabeth Trevor and
her father, James Senior, was a London
haberdasher. She suffered a fair degree
of discrimination at the hands of
male horticulturalists[3] but despite
this won hundreds of prizes for her
orchids, about which she was extremely
knowledgeable and renowned. The Spider
Orchid, *Brassia lawrenciana*, named for
Louisa, and also known as Lawrence's Brassia, is a
South American orchid with spider-like pale yellowish-green flowers.
It is also known as *Brassia cochleata*.

In 1828 Louisa married a surgeon, William Lawrence, who was
twenty years older than her, and this marriage allowed her to develop
her horticultural interests unhindered by a need to earn a living. She
pursued her interests at their homes, first at Drayton Green and later
at Ealing Park, both near London, though her husband remained for
the most part at his house in central London.[3] The Drayton garden was
small but she still managed to grow more than 4000 different species,
including 227 different orchids. By 1838, when her husband purchased
Ealing Park with 100 acres, Louisa had gained 53 Horticultural Society
medals (it did not become 'Royal' until 1861). It was at Ealing Park
that she entertained Queen Victoria and Prince Albert. There was a

race among English horticulturists to produce the first flower of a tree from Burma called *Amherstia nobilis.* Mrs Lawrence succeeded, much to the dismay of the men who were unsuccessful, including the Duke of Northumberland. The plant was transferred to Kew a year before Louisa died and was painted by Marianne North who also features in this book.[4] Louisa was so well known as a horticulturalist that books were dedicated to her.

BOTANICAL NAME
Brassia lawrenceana
COMMON NAME
Spider Orchid
FAMILY
Orchidaceae
NATIVE OF
South America

It was after her death that Jane Loudon, wife of the editor of *The Gardener's Magazine,* wrote in 1858 in her book *The Ladies' Companion to the Flower Garden,* the following dedication *'to the memory of Mrs Lawrence of Ealing Park, Middlesex, one of the first lady-gardeners of her day.'*[5] In addition, Volume 68 of *Curtis's Botanical Magazine,* the work of Sir William Hooker the director of Kew was dedicated *'with sentiments of great regard and esteem'* to Mrs Lawrence, *'the beauty of whose gardens and pleasure grounds and whose most successfully cultivated vegetable treasures are only equalled by the liberality with which they are shown to all who are in botany and horticulture.'*[6] Louisa and William had two sons and two daughters. One son, Sir Trevor Lawrence, became President of the Royal Horticultural Society. Louisa Lawrence exemplified the well-known English female horticulturalists of the time, being decidedly upper class with the means and leisure time to pursue their gardening interests.[7]

Mary Elizabeth Barber (1818-1899)

Mary Elizabeth Barber deserves to be better known outside her adopted South Africa and it is not easy to do her justice in a short biography. She is described as *'probably the most advanced woman of her time in South Africa and contributed many observations on plants and insects.'*[8]

Described as cheerful, self-reliant and with a sense of humour, one of eleven children of Anna Maria Mitford Bowker and Miles Bowker of Deckhams Hall, Gateshead, England, she was born in Wiltshire, but emigrated with her family to South Africa at the age of two.[8] Here the family became well known landowners at a farm called Tharfield.

Mary became very interested in the plants in the area and, despite having no formal training, became a collector and artist. After her marriage in 1845 to Frederick William Barber (1813-92), with whom she had two sons and a daughter, she moved with him to a sheep farm, where she was able to continue her interests in botany while her husband was away on business trips.[9] In 1869 she and her children joined her husband on the diamond fields and they later moved to Johannesburg.

Like many similar such women living abroad, she sent specimens to and corresponded with various well known naturalists in Europe, including Charles Darwin, Joseph Hooker and William Harvey (1811-1866). Harvey was based at Trinity College, Dublin, but spent some years in South Africa. Mary's specimens, those of her brother James and her drawings[10,11] contributed to Harvey's publications, particularly his *Flora Capensis*.[12] Harvey named the genus *Barberetta* in her honour.

She was an illustrator for Joseph Hooker at Kew who regarded her highly and named *Brachystelma barberae* after her. The genus *Bowkeria* is also named after Mary and her brother James and she is commemorated in *Diascia barberae*, pictured here.

Her other interests included entomology, ornithology, fossils and writing poetry. After her husband's death in 1892, she lived with her sons, daughter and brother at their various houses and died at her daughter's home in Pietermaritzburg on 4 September 1899. Shortly before her death her son Frederick had a collection of her poems, *The Erythrina tree and other verses,* published in England.[13]

BOTANICAL NAME
Diascia barberae
COMMON NAME
Twinspur
FAMILY
Scrophulariaceae
NATIVE OF
South Africa

Katherine Saunders (1824-1901)

The plants pictured, and many others, are named for Katherine Saunders, a well know British plant collector and artist. She was the sixth of seven children of Canon Charles Wheelright and was brought up in a tudor-style rectory in Northampton-shire, England.[14] Aged 19 she went to the continent to study drawing and languages.

She met her husband, James Renault Saunders (1818-1892) in Dusseldorf and married him in 1851 at the British Embassy in Brussels. He was born in Mauritius into a trading family and was a co-founder, in 1854, of the Natal Company.

They moved to the Chiappini sugar estate at Tongaat in Natal where Katherine started painting flowers and gardening. Her husband was initially manager and then owner of the estate. Katherine was helped with her botanical interests by Mark John-ston McKen, a Scottish-born botanist who was first manager of the Tongaat Estate before Katherine's husband,

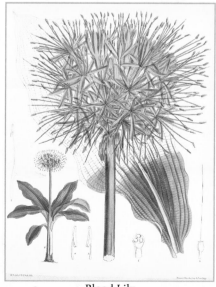

Blood Lily

and then curator of the Durban Botanic Garden, setting up plant exchanges with the UK.

In order to pursue her botanical interests in painting and collecting, Katherine corresponded with Harry Bolus (great-uncle of Harriet Bolus, featured in this book) in Cape Town, William and Joseph Hooker at Kew and William Harvey at Trinity College, Dublin.[8] Later the family moved to Tongaal House which became a centre of botanical activity. Katherine's main interest was in identifying and painting as many native flowers as she could find, particularly those as yet unknown to science.

BOTANICAL NAME
Ornithogalum saundersiae
COMMON NAME
Giant Chincherinchee
FAMILY
Asparaginaceae
NATIVE OF
South Africa

On a visit to England in 1881-2 she brought plants to Kew and continued correspondence with Joseph Hooker and his successor William Thiselton-Dyer until her death in 1901. She received plants from her son, Charles, and from Marianne North (also featured in this book).[8] In total, 426 specimens were sent to Kew between 1881 and 1889 and 16 were named after her or her son, Sir Charles Saunders.

BOTANICAL NAME
Haemanthus katherinae
COMMON NAME
Blood Lily
FAMILY
Amaryllidaceae
NATIVE OF
South Africa

Haemanthus katherinae (also known as *Scadoxus multiflorus*) pictured here, was discovered by her in 1868. Also known by the common name blood lily, *Haemanthus katherinae* has been widely used in mitosis research. Katherine sent bulbs of *Ornithogalum saundersiae* (also pictured here) from South Africa to Kew in 1877.

Other plants named for Katherine include: *Habenaria saundesiae*, *Drimiopsis saundersiae* and *Lisianthus saundersiae*.

Mary Ann Robb (1829-1912)

Mary Ann Robb suffered a number of tragedies in her life. She was the youngest of six children, her mother having died soon after her birth. Despite this, she is reported to have had a happy childhood as part of a large, lively intellectual family with interests in science and technology.[3]

Another tragedy occurred in 1858 when her naval captain husband of two years, John Robb, died leaving her with two young sons. She did not remarry. Her mother was Mary Ann Wilkinson who married Matthew Robinson Boulton, an engineer, who, in 1815, purchased the Tew Park estate in Oxfordshire where she was brought up.[15] In 1808 the then owner of the estate, George Frederick Stratton, had the garden and surrounds set out by John Loudon, the well-known garden designer. Moreover, Mary's grandfather, another Matthew Boulton, was a member of the prestigious Lunar Society, a discussion group of men who met in the Birmingham area to discuss the important issues of the day.[16] The group included such well-known names as Josiah Wedgwood, Erasmus Darwin, James Watt and Joseph Priestley.

Mary's grandfather was a partner with James Watt in the development of the steam engine. With this illustrious background and residence in a park noted for its plants and trees, it is no surprise that Mary took up botany, a subject she enjoyed and which was regarded as being suitable for young women of her station in life. In her later years Mary travelled extensively in search of plants. It was in Turkey (an extension of a trip to Greece) that she found the plant that was subsequently to be named after her – *Euphorbia robbiae* or Mrs Robb's Bonnet.[15,17]

BOTANICAL NAME
Euphorbia robbiae
COMMON NAME
Mrs Robb's Bonnet
FAMILY
Euphorbiaceae
NATIVE OF
Europe

The story of how the plant was named has been widely reported. The tale goes that she found the plant and wanted to transport it back to the UK, but all she had to carry it in was her hat box; no female Victorian adventurer would travel anywhere without somewhere to store her hat. The plant became widely cultivated in gardens following its introduction in 1891, but was not found again in the wild.[17,18] It was through the efforts of E A Bowles (an established plantsman of the time), a friend of Mary's, who grew the plant in his garden in England from which most of the stock of the plant derives.[17] He was responsible for perpetuating the name 'Mrs Robb's Bonnet'.

More recently attempts have been made to determine the botany and genetics of Euphorbia species, of which there are many in Turkey.[18] *Euphorbia robbiae* was designated a new species by William Bertram Turrill in 1953,[19] but was reduced to the sub-species *Euphorbia amygdaloides robbiae* by Alan Radcliffe-Smith in 1976.[20]

In her later years Mary lived at Chitley Place near Liphook in Hampshire, an estate of 150 acres including a renowned garden. She knew Sir William Thiselton-Dyer, the Director of Kew at the time, with whom she corresponded and sent seeds from plants in her garden.

The garden was not maintained by her family after her death in 1912, partly because the outbreak of war in 1914 made this difficult, and the estate was eventually sold in 1929.[15]

Marianne North (1830-90)

Marianne North is probably the best known of the women featured in this book, by virtue of the gallery dedicated to her paintings at Kew Gardens. Her significance in the world of botanical paintings is reflected in the number of plants named after her. As well as *Kniphofia northiae* featured here, she is honoured by, amongst others, *Areca northiana, Crinum northianum, Nepenthes northiana* and the genus *Northia.*[21]

Like many of the important botanical figures of the nineteenth century, she came from a wealthy background and was able to pursue her interests without having to earn a living. She was born in Hastings into a political family, her father, Frederick, being the liberal MP for Hastings and her mother, Janet, the daughter of Sir John Marjoribanks MP. Initially, she trained as a singer but later in life after her voice failed, she took up flower painting, which was considered a respectable hobby for a Victorian lady of leisure.

Her interest in botany was encouraged by her father who introduced her to Sir Joseph Hooker, director of the Royal Botanic Gardens at Kew. After the death of her mother in 1855, she travelled with her father and after his death in 1868 decided to pursue her grand ambition of searching out and painting the flora of the world.[3] She became an intrepid traveller who never married so had no husband or family to limit her journeys to parts of the world not usually on the itinerary of Victorian women. Her travel began in Canada, the USA and Jamaica, followed by a year in Brazil. In 1875, after a few months in Tenerife she began a journey round the world, and for two years painted the flora of California, Japan, Borneo, Java and Ceylon (now Sri Lanka), followed by a year in India.[22] She was seemingly oblivious to the hardships she encountered on her travels which included heat, heavy rains, insects, mud and diseases. On her return to Britain she offered to give her paintings to Kew and provided the funds to build a gallery in the grounds of the garden, which opened in 1882.

She continued to travel until a few years before her death in 1890, visiting Chile and The Seychelles in 1884-5. It is important to note the scientific accuracy of her paintings at a time when photography was in its infancy and not an option for her on her travels. Her paintings depicted plants in the environment in which they were found rather than in the usual manner of drawing on a white background. In 2008 Kew obtained a grant from the National Lottery to undertake a major restoration of both the gallery and the paintings inside, the sight of which, to the visitor, is truly remarkable.

BOTANICAL NAME
Kniphofia northiae
COMMON NAME
Giant Red Hot Poker
FAMILY
Asphodelaceae
NATIVE OF
South Africa

Olga Aleksandrovna Fedchenko (1845-1921)

Olga Aleksandrovna Fedchenko (née Armfeld) was a well-known, largely self-taught Russia botanist and plant collector after whom many plants, including *Rosa fedtschenkoana* (pictured), *Incarvillea olgae*, and *Eremurus olgae* were named.[23] She was a world renowned expert on the flora of Turkestan where she undertook several challenging expeditions, often on horseback. She was born in Moscow into a large, well-respected family and initially trained as an artist. The family's summer residence outside Moscow was where she developed her botanical interests. The garden, containing many of the plants she had collected during her travels, was destroyed by Bolsheviks in 1921.

The herbarium compiled when she was just 16 years of age was used in the *Moskovskaia Flora* by Nikolai Kaufman, a considerable achievement for a woman with no formal botanical training. Her marriage in 1867 to Aleksei Fedchenko (1844-1873), a naturalist and explorer, whom she had met whilst helping him at the Moscow Zoological Museum, was tragically short lived when he died in an accident on Mount Blanc just six years later, leaving her with a young son, Boris.[24] Olga had taken part in her husband's expedition to Turkestan in 1868-71 where her expertise in the flora of the region was established.

After the death of her husband, Olga continued her botanical work, becoming the second female member-correspondent of the Russian Academy of Sciences and subsequently an honorary fellow. In later life she undertook further expeditions to Turkestan in 1901, 1910 and 1915, together with her son, also a botanist, who became the chief curator of the Turkestan Herbarium at the St. Petersburg Imperial Botanic Garden.

BOTANICAL NAME
Rosa fedtschenkoana
COMMON NAME
Fedtschenko Rose
FAMILY
Rosaceae
NATIVE OF
Asia

They had moved to St. Petersburg in 1900. She was also well-known outside Russia and corresponded with other botanists and gardens, including Kew. She had interests in plant classification and systematics, particularly in the genera *Eremurus* and *Iris* and her legacy is important in demonstrating that women are as capable as men of undertaking demanding expeditions to largely unexplored areas of the world.

Marianne Harriet Mason (1845-1932)

Marianne Harriet Mason was a woman of many talents. Although she was English and spent most of her life in England, it was in South Africa that she made her plant discoveries. Not only was she a respected botanical artist and plant collector, she also collected and published traditional folk songs[25,26] and became the first inspector of boarded out children under the local government board (i.e. the first female civil servant), a job she performed for thirty years in England.[27]

She was born in London into an aristocratic family, her father, George Mason, being a lawyer. When she was a child the family, of which she was the eldest of seven, moved to Wales, then to Morton Hall, Retford. Two years were spent in Switzerland and it was here that Marianne's interest in alpine plants developed and in which she became an authority. After retiring from her civil service post, Marianne moved to South Africa to be with her brother, Canon George Mason who was principal of St. Bede's College in Umtata. While there she explored the area collecting plants, painting and discovered new plants that were named after her: *Crocosmia masonorum* (Iridaceae) (pictured here), *Watsonia masoniae* (Iridaceae), *Nerine maso-*

Small Alpine Nerine

niorum (Amaryllidaceae) and *Indigofera masoniae* (Fabaceae). The first three in the list were named by Louise Bolus who appears elsewhere in this book. According to Gunn & Codd's *Botanical Exploration of Southern Africa*, Marianne *'made leisurely journeys by cart and horses to out-of-the-way places'* collecting seeds and bulbs and painting plants in South Africa.[8] On her return to England in 1912, she exhibited some of her paintings (of which there were about 400) which were eventually acquired by Kew, along with her books of plant studies. The black and white picture of the Nerine (shown on the opposite page) is from one of

Marianne's paintings which appeared in her paper published in 1913.[28] The paper begins with the words *'This sketch is intended to be neither botanical nor horticultural but simply descriptive of the flowers as they grew wild in their own home,'* and describes in some insightful detail her travels in search of flowers.[28]

It also mentions the *Montbretia* in the herbarium of Mrs F Bolus (i.e. Louisa Bolus who features in this book). After the war, Marianne returned to South Africa where she built a house near Cape Town and died there in 1932.

BOTANICAL NAME
Crocosmia masonorum
COMMON NAME
Giant Montbretia
FAMILY
Iridaceae
NATIVE OF
South Africa

Antoinette Emily Danford (1851-1927)

Antoinette Emily Danford (née Dyce) is usually referred to as Mrs Charles Danford with her first names being hardy ever recorded. She was born in 1851 in Aberdeen, Scotland.

She and Charles had a son, Bertram William Young Danford, born in 1875, who had a distinguished army career.

She was a plant explorer and wife of the lawyer, artist and ornithologist Charles George Danford (1843-1928). *Iris danfordiae* is found in the mountains of Turkey where it flowers near the snowline. This yellow dwarf Iris was found in 1876 by Antoinette who was the first person to introduce it to England. It may not flower reliably in the second and third years, but if buried deep and left undisturbed, it will recover and naturalise by bulblet. *Crocus danfordiae*, again from Turkey, is also named after her.

She died in France in 1927 and is buried in Aberdeen.[29,30]

> **BOTANICAL NAME**
> *Iris danfordiae*
> **COMMON NAME**
> Buttercup Iris
> **FAMILY**
> Iridaceae
> **NATIVE OF**
> Turkey

Matilda Smith (1854-1926)

Matilda Smith was born in Bombay but moved to England as a child.[2] Little is known about her family but she had influential relatives: notably, she was the second cousin of Joseph Dalton Hooker, Director of Kew (1865-85).

Although she had no formal botanical training she loved plants and her interest was encouraged by her cousin. She joined Kew at the age of 23 and over the following 40 years contributed many drawings to *Curtis's Botanical Magazine*. By 1887 she was one of the few botanical artists working for the magazine. However, it was not until 1898 that she was officially recognised as the sole official artist for *Curtis's*.[2,7] She worked closely with botanists when drawing a specimen, and her detailed drawings were of practical appeal to them as well as to horticulturalists and gardeners.

Between 1878 and 1923, she drew over 2,300 plates for *Curtis's* and other publications, including *Transactions of the Linnaean Society, The Royal Society* and the *Kew Guild*. She became President of the last-named in 1916 and was also an Associate of the Linnaean Society (1921): only the second woman to have been appointed. She was awarded the Veitch Memorial Medal of the Royal Horticultural Society and contributed drawings to Joseph Hooker's New Zealand Flora,[31] and to his *Icones Plantarum* [32] (Illustrations of Plants) which were drawn from Kew's herbarium specimens.

Matilda never married and is buried in Richmond cemetery, near London. Her cousin, Joseph Hooker is buried in St. Anne's Church, Kew. His memorial plaque in the church was designed by Matilda and features a design of five plants. Three years after her death, negative comments about her work were made by Wilfrid Blunt in his book of botanical illustrations,[33] but her drawings belie such comments and she had many supportive friends.

Plant genera, *Smithiantha* and *Smithiella* were named in her honour.

BOTANICAL NAME
Smithiantha cinnabarina
COMMON NAME
Temple Bells
FAMILY
Gesneriaceae
NATIVE OF
Mexico

Ellen Ann Willmott (1858-1934)

Ellen Willmott was an internationally known, enigmatic, very wealthy woman who used her fortune to pursue her interests in gardening and plants.[3,7,34] Her wealth came from two sources. Firstly, her parents, Frederick (a solicitor) and Ellen Willmott purchased Warley Place in Essex in 1875, an estate with 33 acres of grounds. As the eldest of three daughters, Ellen inherited the house after her mother's death and lived there all of her life. Secondly, Ellen also received a large inheritance on the death of her godmother, which allowed her to buy a chateau known as Tresserve near Aix-les-Bains in France in 1890 which unfortunately burnt down in 1907. In 1905 she also purchased Boccanegra, an Italian estate which had one of several gardens of English design in the area, just over the border from the French Riviera.

BOTANICAL NAME
Ceratostigma willmottianum
COMMON NAME
Chinese Plumbago
FAMILY
Plumbaginaceae
NATIVE OF
China

Intriguing correspondence between Ellen and Clarence Bricknell, an Englishman who settled in Italy and built Casa Fontanalba in the nearby town of Bordighera, shed a somewhat different light on Ellen's character. The letters mainly discussed plants and seeds that might be used to develop Ellen's garden since Clarence was a botanical expert as well as having interests in art and archaeology. Clarence was able to chide Ellen gently for being a poor correspondent at the same time as appreciating her business.[35] Ellen visited her overseas properties only twice a year. Eventually her high level of spending, which included the employment of over 100 gardeners, led to later financial problems; she had to sell her overseas properties and many of her personal possessions.

Her eccentricity increased as she aged, prompting her to carry a gun and fit alarms at her estate, and she was known to be a difficult employer. After her death, and with no heirs, Warley Place was sold to pay her debts and demolished in 1939. In contrast, Boccanegra remains and can still be visited. At her peak Ellen is said to have cultivated more than 100,000 species and varieties of plants. She received numerous honours; she was one of only two women (the other being Gertrude Jekyll) to receive the RHS Victoria

Warley Place

Medal when it was inaugurated in 1897. She was also one of the first women to be elected a Fellow of the Linnaean Society of London, in 1905. She was an enthusiastic funder of plant-hunting expeditions including some of those of E.H. Wilson to China. *Ceratostigma willmottianum* is one of over sixty plants named for her. The garden at Warley Place is now a nature reserve.

Harriet Margaret Louisa Bolus (1877-1970)

One of the few women in this book to live into the twentieth century, Louisa Bolus (née Kensit) was a South African botanist and taxonomist who specialised in the genus *Mesembryanthemum* and devoted her life to the herbarium which she took over after the death of her great-uncle Harry Bolus in 1903.[14]

She was born in Burgersdorp, South Africa, the daughter of William Kensit and Jane Stuart and was educated at the Girls' Collegiate School, Port Elizabeth and the South African College, Cape Town, graduating with a BA (Litt.).[8] In 1912 she married Frank Bolus who was her father's cousin and Harry Bolus's son. In his will, Harry left his herbarium and botanical library to what was to become the University of Cape Town with funds to maintain and extend it. However, a condition of the bequest was that Louisa should continue as its curator. She fulfilled the terms of her great-uncle's will, finally retiring in 1955 at the age of 77 to become Honorary Reader at the University of Cape Town and continued her taxonomic work; quite an achievement for a woman and someone without any formal botanical training.

When younger, Louisa collected plants locally but had to stop when she suffered an injury to her ankle. She died in 1970 at the age of 93 as one of the best known South African botanists. During her long life she received numerous awards, including an Honorary Doctorate of Science from Stellenbosch University, Fellowship of the Royal Society of South Africa and Fellowship of the Linnaean Society.

BOTANICAL NAME
Bolusanthemum tugwelliae
COMMON NAME
Prince Albert Vygie
FAMILY
Aizoaceae
NATIVE OF
South Africa

She published and edited many books, including *Elementary lessons in systematic botany based on familiar species of the South African flora* (Cape Town, 1919), a school textbook, reflecting her background as a teacher and enthusiasm in promoting the study of plants by children.[36] There was also *A book of South African flowers* (Cape Town, 1925) and *A second book of South African flowers* (Cape Town, 1936). She was not an artist, so others illustrated her books. Her taxonomic interest led her to name many new genera, including *Leipoldtia, Esterhuysenia* and *Peersia*, amongst others. Her name lives on in two genera (*Kensitia* and *Bolusanthemum*) and in a number of species (e.g. *Conophytum bolusiae, Ruschia bolusiae, Moraea louisabolusiae*) and others.[37]

Helen Milford (1877-1940)

Helen A Milford was a horticulturalist who collected plants in the Drakensberg Mountains of South Africa and introduced them into England.[37] She visited the mountains in 1936 and 1938-9 and collected living plants to propagate at her alpine nursery in Chedworth, Gloucestershire. The alpine plant *Crassula milfordii* was also named after her.

BOTANICAL NAME
Helicrysum milfordii
COMMON NAME
None
FAMILY
Asteraceae
NATIVE OF
South Africa

She was the first great plant collector of the Drakensberg in the 1930s and 1940s. Little more is known of her and there is no picture.

References

1. Aitken, R. *Botanical Riches: Stories of Botanical Exploration.* Melbourne University Publishing, Singapore, 2007.

2. Kramer, J. *Women of Flowers.* Welcome Books, New York, 2005.

3. Horwood, C. *Gardening Women,* Virago, London, 2010.

4. Campbell-Culver, M̂. *The Origin of Plants.* Transworld Publishers, London, 2001.

5. Loudon, J. *The Ladies' Companion to the Flower Garden, being an Alphabetical Arrangement of all the ornamental plants usually grown in gardens and shrubberies, with full directions for their culture.* Bradbury & Evans, London, 1858.

6. Curtis's Botanical Magazine, 68 (1842-1920).

7. Penn, H. *An Englishwoman's Garden.* BBC Books, London, 1993.

8. Gunn, M. & Codd, L.E. *Botanical Exploration of Southern Africa.* Botanical Research Institute Cape Town, 1981.

9. Cohen, A. *Mary Elizabeth Barber: South Africa's first lady natural historian.* Archives of Natural History. 27 (2), 187-208, 2000.

10. S2A3, *Mary Elizabeth Barber.* Biographical Database of South African Science, 1972.

11. Mitford-Barberton, I. *The Barbers of the Peak.* Oxford University Press, Oxford, 1934.

12. Harvey, W.H. & Sonder, A. *Flora Capensis.* A. Robertson, Cape Town, 1859.

13. Barber, M.E. *The Erythrina Tree and Other Verses.* R. Ward, London, 1898.

14. Creese, M.R.S & Creese, T.M. *Ladies in the Laboratory III: South African, Australian, New Zealand, and Canadian Women in Science,* page 5. The Scarecrow Press Inc., Plymouth, 2010.

15. Haines, C.M.C. *International Women in Sciences: a Biographical Dictionary to 1950.* ABC Clio, Oxford, 2001.

16. Lunar Society. www.lunarsociety.org.uk

17. Stearn, W.T. *Mrs Robb and Mrs Robb's Bonnet.* J. Roy. Hort. Soc, 98, 306-310, 1973.

18. Can, L., Erol, O., Challen, G. & Kucuker, O. *On the rediscovery of Euphorbia amygdaloides subsp. robbiae and its type.* Turk. J. Bot. 36, 650-654, 2012.

19. Turrill, W.B. *Euphorbia robbiae.* Curtis's Botanical Magazine, 169, 208, 1953.

20. Radcliffe-Smith, A. *The mystery of Euphorbia robbiae (Euphorbiaceae).* Kew Bulletin, 30, 697-8, 1976.

21. Encyclopaedia of World Biography. *Marianne North.* The Gale Group, 2004.

22. North, M. *A Vision of Eden: The Life and Work of Marianne North,* Holt, Rinehard and Winston, 1980.

23. *Fedtschenko, Aleksei Pavlovich (Alexei Pawlowitsch)* (1844–1873)'. plants. jstor.org.

24. Crease, M.R.S. *Ladies in the Laboratory IV. Russia's Women in Science 1800-1900,* page 71.

25. *Old Songs and Sugar Mice: the story of the remarkable Miss Mason.* www. thefreelibrary.com

26. Mason, M. *Nursery Rhymes and Country Songs,* Metzler, London, 1877.

27. *Miss Marianne H. Mason, First Inspector of Boarded Out Children under the Local Government Board.* http://artuk.org

28. Mason, M.H. *Some Flowers of Central and Eastern Africa.* J. Roy. Hort. Soc. 39, 8-16, 1913.

29. www.soldiersofthequeen.com/HomeService-BertramDanfordRoy-alEngineers.html

30. www.rootspoint.com

31. Hooker, J.D. *Handbook of New Zealand Flora.* Government of New Zealand, Reeve & Co., London, 1867.

32. Hooker, J. D. *Icones Plantarum.* Dulau & Co., London, 1901.

33. Blunt, W. *The Art of Botanical Illustration.* Collins, London, 1950.

34. Le Lièvre, A. *Miss Willmott of Warley Place.* Faber & Faber, London, 1980.

35. Bicknell, S. *Letters from Clarence Bicknell to Ellen Willmott between 1902-1916 –Boccanegra Gardens.* www.clarencebicknell.com

36. S2A3 Biographical Database of Southern African Science. *Biography of Louisa Bolus.*

37. The Eponym Dictionary of Southern African Plants: Plant Names A-B www.calflora.net

CHAPTER
•FOUR•

THE TWENTIETH CENTURY

> **Kathleen Kellogg Meserve** (1906-1999)
>
> **Margaret Ursula Mee** (1909-1988)

By the twentieth century industrial expansion had reached its peak and plant hunting was in decline, but not entirely lost[1]. However, just two women out of the selection for this book lived entirely in the twentieth century.

One was American and the other British and their approaches to botany and horticulture were very different. Kathleen Meserve was self- taught and achieved great acclaim by patenting her hybrid hollies which, in contrast to other hollies, were hardy enough to survive the harsh winters of the eastern United States. In contrast, Margaret Mee, although British, spent much of her life in Brazil as a botanical artist and plant hunter and she, too, received much acclaim during her life. The difference between these two women, and those of earlier centuries who were less recognised for their work, may be a reflection of the development of the written and spoken word - in radio, television, books, and towards the end of their lives, the internet and digital media. Biographies of the two women follow.

Kathleen Kellogg Meserve (1906- 1999)

The American Kathleen Kellogg Meserve is unusual amongst the group of women in this book in that she lived entirely in the twentieth century, dying in 1999 in Florida aged 93. She was proud of having no formal horticultural training yet became well known in her lifetime for her hybrid hollies which were sold around the world. In fact some of the information for this account of her life is taken from various obituaries, notably in the New York Times[2] and the Chicago Tribune,[3] a reflection of her horticultural and national standing.

The former Kathleen Kellogg was born in Manhattan, New York City but her family moved to a ten acre estate on Long Island after World War II, so she had the resources to pursue her interest in hollies which she had first heard about from a garden club lecture. Her husband, F. Leighton Meserve died in 1968 and she did not remarry. She found that the holly, *Ilex aquifolium*, sold at Christmas in the Eastern USA, but which succumbed to the harsh winters in cultivation, could be crossed with *Ilex rugosa*, a native of Japan, to produce what became known as blue hollies which were hardy enough to be grown locally. They were named *Ilex x meserveae* after Kathleen. The blue holly hybrids which have dark, glossy pointed blue-green leaves, became very popular and were initially marketed by Conard-Pyle Nurseries of Michigan, USA. They were patented[4] and the proceeds of their sale allowed Kathleen to maintain her estate, known as Holly-By-Golly.[5]

She received numerous honours, including one from the United States Patent Office in 1980 on the 50th anniversary of the Plant Patent Law for her contributions to horticulture, and further awards from the American Horticultural Society in 1975 and from the Royal Horticultural Society in 1992. She is reported as being surprised by her success and to relish the fact that she had no horticultural training yet, at one point she held more plant patents than any other person in the USA.

BOTANICAL NAME
Ilex x meserveae
COMMON NAME
Blue Holly
FAMILY
Aquifoliaceae
NATIVE OF
Most parts of the World

Of the many cultivars of her hollies, 'Blue Boy' and 'Blue Girl' introduced in 1964, were the most successful.[4] However, *Ilex x meserveae* is generally known simply as Blue Holly.

Margaret Ursula Mee (1909-1988)

Margaret Ursula Mee, like Kathleen Meserve, also lived entirely in the 20th century She is well known as a botanical artist and plant hunter who spent much of her life in Brazil, exploring and plant hunting in the rain forest and painting in gouache from specimens in their natural habitats.[6]

She is one of the most celebrated female plant hunters and artists of her generation and received much acclaim during her life, unlike many women with similar interests before her.[6]

The photograph of Margaret reproduced here was taken on the Rio Negro in Brazil in May 1988 on the day she painted the Moonflower in what was to be her last expedition, when she was 78.[7] The Moonflower *(Selenicereus wittii)*, is a rare cactus which has flowers that open only at night and Margaret had long wanted to paint it. She was born Margaret Ursula Brown in Chesham, England, a rural area with little access to schools so was educated at home mainly by her mother's sister Ellen Mary Churchman who was a children's book illustrator. After the First World she went to school in Amersham, England where her artistic abilities were first noticed. Her father was also interested in natural history and she spent time with him observing wild flowers and learning their names. Her first husband, Reg Bartlett, was a trade union activist alongside whom she campaigned on workers' rights and unemployment. After they divorced she later married Greville Mee, a commercial artist, whom she met at St. Martin's School of Art in London.[8] Together they visited Brazil to see Margaret's sister, Catherine, who was ill. As a result of this visit Margaret's interest in the flora of Brazil came to the fore such that she spent most of the rest of her life there, undertaking 15 expeditions into the rainforest over a 35 year period.

Margaret received numerous awards including the Grenfell Medal of the Royal Horticultural Society in 1960 (for watercolour painting) and an MBE in 1976. Her seemingly frail exterior belied an inner determination. However, having survived various diseases including malaria and hepatitis as well as the ravages of numerous insects and other pests she died, ironically, in a car crash in England in 1988.[9] Funds gathered in her memory have been used to finance Brazilian botanists to attend courses at Kew to promote the continuation of botanical exploration in the country.

In 1980 a large format book, *Flores do Amazonas (Flowers of the Amazon)*, containing 24 plates of Margaret's paint-

BOTANICAL NAME
Sobralia margaretae
COMMON NAME
None
FAMILY
Bromeliaceae
NATIVE OF
Brazil

ings of Brazilian plants, was initially published in Portuguese.[10] It was beautifully printed with a gold-embossed green case and included descriptions of the plants, a map of Amazonia indicating where they could be found, and an English translation of the text. The idea was that the book should be given as a gift to diplomats and government visitors to Brazil as a showcase of the country and of the Amazon. Only 1000 numbered copies were printed and now they fetch high prices when they appear on the market.

The painting of the orchid *Sobralia margaretae*, illustrating the work of Margaret and reproduced here, is from the book. The orchid was identified as a new species by Guido Pabst in 1977 and named after Margaret.[7]

Another of the plants named after Margaret, *Neoregelia margaretae* is a member of the Bromeliad family which grows as an epiphyte on plants and trees in the Brazilian rainforest. The plant was named in 1968 by Lyman Bradford Smith who was a world authority on Bromeliads and worked at the

Sobralia margaretae

Smithsonian in Washington helping to develop Margaret's knowledge of these plants.

Neoregelia rosea

The plant *Neoregelia margaretae* collects moisture and water droplets that form a pool in the centre of the leaf that acts as an ecosystem for other plants and small insects and is the site of plant debris accumulation. The plants extract nutrients from this debris to support growth since they do not have ground roots but grow on other plants and trees as epiphytes.[6] The picture shown here is *Neoregelia rosea* which is similar to *Neoregelia margaretae.* Other plants named after Margaret are *Aechmea meeana* and *Nidularium meeanum.*

References

1. Short, P. *In Pursuit of Plants.* Timber Press, Cambridge, 2004.

2. Honan, W.H. *Kathleen K. Meserve*, 93, bred holly hybrids. New York Times, 30 May, 1999. http://www.nytimes.com

3. Chicago Tribune. *Holly Hybridist Kathleen Meserve.* May 30, 1999. http://articles.chicagotribune.com

4. Stanley, A. *Mothers and Daughters of Invention.* Rutgers University Press, New Brunswick, 1995.

5. Laurries Blogspot. *Holly by Golly.* 14.12.10. http://laurries.blogspot.co.uk

6. Mabey, R. *The Cabaret of Plants: Botany and the Imagination.* Profile Books Ltd., London, 2015.

7. Morrison, T. *Margaret Mee's Amazon,* www.nonsuchexpeditions.com, 1987.

8. Kramer, J. *Women of Flowers.* Welcome Books, New York, 1996.

9. Vines, G. *Drawn to the Rainforest. Kew Magazine,* RBG, Kew, London, Spring 2016.

10. Mee, M. *Flores do Amazonas – Flowers of the Amazon.* Distribuidora Record de Servicios da Imprensa S.A., Rio de Janiero, Brazil, 1980.

CHAPTER
•FIVE•

The Oregon Connection

Almeda Zibia Barrett (1831-1924)

Nancy Jane Davis (1833-1921)

Lilla Leach (1886-1980)

Oregon in the Pacific North-West of the USA is a beautiful area with high mountains, wilderness, a dramatic coastline and a small population. Oregon was the 33rd state to be admitted to the union of the United States, in 1859. In 1850 it had a population of just 12,093, but by 1860 this had increased to 52,465.[1] The population then gradually increased year on year to reach 4,028,977 by 2015.

At this stage it was the 39th state in terms of population density with 40.9 people per square mile but the 9th largest in terms of area. For such a sparsely populated area of the USA to produce three women with plants named after them is unusual and prompted me to assign them a chapter of their own.

The terrain of Oregon is varied and mountainous as well as densely wooded in parts, providing excellent hunting grounds for new and unusual plants, particularly at the time when the three women, Almeda Barrett, Nancy Davis and Lilla Leach were active in the 19th and early

20th centuries. Almeda Barrett was associated with the Hood River area of Oregon and Lilla Leach lived on the outskirts of Portland, the largest city in the state. The picture (below left) shows the former volcano, Mount Hood, snow–capped even in August. The second picture shows a flower meadow in the Mount Hood area.

Mount Hood   Oregon countryside

Nancy Davis did not live in Oregon but collected plants growing from Northern California and extending into Oregon and is therefore included in this chapter. Nancy and Almeda were contemporaries, though there is no evidence they knew each other. Both communicated with the well-known American botanist Professor Asa Gray.

Lilla Leach collected her plants at a later date than Almeda and Nancy and extended her activities well into the twentieth century. The house and garden owned by Lilla Leach and her husband John is known as the 'Leach Botanical Garden' or 'Portland's Secret Garden' after being left to the City of Portland by the couple after their deaths. It is now run as a not-for-profit organisation.[2] It features a collection of over 2000 plant species with garden tours, special events, programmes and classes. It is supported by local businesses and individuals and has free entry. I visited the garden in 2014 and discovered that neither the hotel receptionist in Portland nor the taxi driver had heard of it – it is a secret garden! However, the visit was most interesting with the garden and buildings providing a wealth of information about Lilla and John and their lives. The house itself is an attractive clapboard structure with a shop selling books by John and the garden is a deep wooded area around the banks of Johnson Creek with rambling pathways and vistas revealing a wide range of trees, shrubs and herbaceous plants. At the time of my visit in late summer the two *Kalmiopsis leachiana* plants located near the shop were unfortunately not in flower, the flowering period being in the late spring. Further information about Lilla Leach can be found later in this chapter.

Johnson Creek

Kalmiopsis leachiana

Lilla Leach's house

97

Almeda Zabia Barrett (1831-1924)

Penstemon barrettiae is named for its collector, Almeda Zabia Barrett (born Hodge) of Hood River, Oregon, USA. With her husband Dr. Perry Gordon Barrett and daughter Julia, she settled in the Hood River Valley in 1871.[3] Barrett Spur on Mt. Hood was named for Dr Perry Barrett who for many years was the only physician in the valley.

They lived close to the site of Barrett School, and at one time all the west side of the Hood River Valley was known as the Barrett District. Even today there is a Barrett Drive and Barrett Park in the town of Hood River.

BOTANICAL NAME
Penstemon barrettiae
COMMON NAME
Barrett's Beardtongue
FAMILY
Plantaginaceae
NATIVE OF
USA (Washington and Oregon)

Almeda Barrett was a keen botanist and enthusiastically sought out new and rare plants. Professor Asa Gray (1810-1888), author and well-known American botanist named *Penstemon barrettiae* after her when she sent him a specimen for identification.

Almeda's daughter Julia attended the Barrett School then went to Rochester, New York to attend college and afterwards to Wellesley

College. Mr and Mrs Hodge (Almeda's parents) moved to Hood River to be near Dr and Mrs Barrett after their daughter, Julia, left home. However, tragedy followed for, after her marriage to Oliver Howell and a move to Honduras, Julia contracted 'Honduras fever' (possibly malaria). She came back to Hood River but died in 1892 at the age 23 leaving twin sons in the care of Almeda and her husband, Perry.[4]

The Barretts kept Jersey cows which Perry Barrett greatly enjoyed. However, one morning in 1900, while tending to his herd, he dropped dead from heart failure aged 70 years. Almeda then moved with her grandsons to New York, where she died in 1924 aged 92 years and is buried in Buffalo.

Penstemon barrettiae is rare, being found only along ten miles of the Columbia River Gorge and along the upper Klickitat River in Oregon.[5] There are no pictures of Almeda Barrett.

Nancy Jane Davis (1833-1921)

Nancy Jane Davis is another female botanist whose identity was a mystery until 1926 when a chance conversation revealed who she was.

The American botanist John Torrey (1796-1873) named *Leucothoe davisiae* after Nancy in 1867. It is a shrub that is toxic to both humans and animals[6] and was discovered by Nancy near the town of Eureka in Northern California in 1863. Its range is now known to extend into southern Oregon which is the reason Nancy is included in this chapter even though she did not live in Oregon.[1]

It was the American botanist, Asa Gray (1810-1888) who published the name of the plant in 1867.[7] Jepson's account in 1934 identified Nancy as a botanist and founder of the Birmingham School (now the Grier School) in Birmingham, Pennsylvania.[8]

The story is that in 1926 a group of botanists were chatting in a garden in New York State when one of them (Professor Joseph Horace Faull (1870-1961), a plant collector of Toronto University) mentioned the name Nancy Davis. This encouraged further investigation and solved the mystery of her identity.

It emerged that Nancy was born near Lewiston, Pennsylvania, USA and at the age of 20 years was one of the founders of Birmingham

School and its principal for over 60 years.[9] She was a graduate of Mount Holyoke College who awarded her a doctorate on the 60th anniversary of the school's foundation. She visited California on a number of occasions to carry out botanical investigations sending her collection of plants mainly to Asa Gray. She also spent some time at the University of Cambridge in England. Another plant, *Polygonum davisiae*, (Davis's Knotweed, now known as *Aconogonon davisiae*), and found in northern California and southern Oregon, was also named after her by the American botanist William Henry Brewer (1828-1910) in 1872.[10]

BOTANICAL NAME
Leucothoe davisiae
COMMON NAME
Sierra Laurel
FAMILY
Ericaceae
NATIVE OF
USA: Oregon and California

Lilla Leach (1886-1980)

Kalmiopsis leachiana, a dwarf evergreen shrub with pink flowers, was discovered in Oregon in 1930 by Lilla Leach of Portland, Oregon's largest city. As described earlier, Portland is also home to the Leach Botanical Garden which is on the site of the house and garden purchased in 1931 where Lilla and her husband John lived.

She was born Lilla Irvin but her mother died shortly after her birth; her father subsequently remarried and her childhood was happy. She attended the University of Oregon where she pursued her botanical interests, eventually becoming a science teacher in Eugene, Oregon. Meanwhile, Lilla's future husband, John, whom she had first met at school, became a pharmacist and settled in Portland.[11] They married in 1913 and began going on botanising expeditions in the Oregon countryside.

In a book about his own life, John wrote *'We found 15 species and two new genera'*. He also wrote at the front of the book *'To Lilla, my wife, who is more than a wife. She's a friend. She doesn't know I've written this while she's in her study poring over her plant lore. But the first copy goes to her'.*[11]

Lilla's contributions to botany did not go unnoticed in the wider world. She was a winner of the American Award for Botany and, in 1950, the first to receive the Eloise Payne Luquer bronze medal awarded by the Garden Clubs of America.[12] Since 1962 the area where Lilla discovered *Kalmiopsis Leachiana* has been dedicated by the United States Forest Service as a botanical preserve called The Big Craggies Botanical Area.

The Leaches were public spirited and in their wills left their house, known as Sleepy Hollow, to the City of Portland as a botanical park and museum. To this day it is a well loved garden on the edge of Portland with free admission, and puts on numerous activities and events; it is a fitting tribute to Lilla and her important contributions to plant science.

The garden has a very informative website (www.leachgarden.org) from which some of the material for this biography was gathered and where more details about Lilla and her life are recorded.

BOTANICAL NAME
Kalmiopsis leachiana
COMMON NAME
None
FAMILY
Ericaceae
NATIVE OF
USA: Oregon

References

1. US Census Data.

2. Leach Botanical Garden leaflet. Portland Parks and Recreation, 2014

3. www.findagrave.com

4. www.historichoodriver.com *The Barrett Twins.*

5. www.science.halleyhosting.com

6. Tucker,G.C. *Leucothoe davisiae* Torrey ex. A Gray. Flora of North America, JStor Global Plants.

7. Gray, A. Proc. Am. Acad. Arts and Science 7, 400, 1867.

8. Jepson, L.W. *The Botanical Explorers of California* IX. Madrona, 2 (14), 115-8, 1934.

9. Green, H. *The Grier School. The first hundred years.* 1953, The Grier School, Pennsylvania, USA.

10. Freeman C.C. *Aconogonon davisiae* (W. H. Brewer ex A. Gray) Soják var. Glabrum (G. N. Jones) S. P. Hong [family Polygonaceae]. Jstor Global Plants.

11. Leach, J.R. *Ox Bows and Bare Feet.* Leach Botanic Garden, Portland, Oregon, 1952.

12. Kirkpatrick, G., Holzwarth, C. and Mullens, L. *The Botanist and her Muleskinner.* Leach Garden Friends, Portland, Oregon, 1994.

CHAPTER
•SIX•

The Ones That
(Almost) Got Away

Maria de Brimeur

Miss Burgess

Mrs R.V. Butt

Mme. Coignet

Jeanne Daigremont

The women in this chapter are those who cannot be fitted into the chronology of earlier chapters because their dates are unknown. Very little information has been found about any of these women; what has been unearthed is outlined in this chapter. All appear to have been botanists or collectors in their own right rather than having plants named after them by their husbands and so are included here.

In some instances, even their first name is unknown and they are simply referred to by their husband's name or as Miss or Mme X. It is very surprising that women who have had the accolade of having plants named after them should be so little known, but this is obviously a reflection of the times in which they lived. Precisely when they lived has to be inferred from other dates, such as that when their plant was discovered or named. One of the women, Maria de Brimeur, lived in the 16th century making her one of the earliest women to feature in this book. She is also one of two women in this chapter whose first name is known, the other being Jeanne Daigremont. Jeanne lived in the 19th century, as did Miss Burgess, Mrs Butt and Mme Coignet.

Only two of the women in this group, Miss Burgess and Mrs Butt (probably), were British, the others being Belgian (Maria de Brimeur) and French (Mme Coignet and Jeanne Daigremont). Maria de Brimeur was a botanist and the other four horticulturalists.

The plants after which they are named come from very different parts of the world: Maria de Brimeur (Europe), Miss Burgess (Tanzania), Mrs Butt (Colombia), Mme Coignet (Japan) and Jeanne Daigremont (Madagascar). This chapter brings these women together, listed in alphabetical order. Unfortunately there are no pictures of them.

Maria de Brimeur

Brimeura is a genus of herbaceous monocot. bulbs with only three species, originally included in the genus *Hyacinthus*. In appearance the flowers are rather like bluebells. In 1866 they were allocated to a separate genus, *Brimeura*, by Richard A Salisbury, a British botanist, in order to honour Maria de Brimeur who was a plant enthusiast and gardener in 16th century Belgium.

Little is known about Maria although one account mentions her marriage to Conrad Schetz who was responsible for promoting the distribution of the bulbs in Belgium and died in 1579.[1]

She is also mentioned by Carolus Clusius (1526-1609) in *Rariorum plantarum historia* (1601)[2] and in *Rariorum aliquot Stirpium per Hispanias observatarum historia* (1576)[3]; both important botanical volumes at the time.

The same account states that Maria was the daughter of Jacques de Brimeu, Lord of Poederlee.[1] All that can be said is that she was a Belgian (or possibly French) botanist who lived in Antwerp during the 16th century for at least part of her life.

BOTANICAL NAME
Brimeura amethystina
COMMON NAME
Amethyst Hyacinth
FAMILY
Asparagaceae
NATIVE OF
Southern Europe

Miss Burgess

Miss Burgess of Birkenhead was reported to be a friend of William T Gerrard, formerly of Liverpool, who moved to Durban, South Africa,[4] but little else is known of her.

Gerrard (died 1865) was English and a very keen collector, especially of trees, and is commemorated in the names of many Natal plants. He arrived in Natal in 1856, remaining for eight years. He and Mark Johnston McKen (curator of the Durban Botanic Garden) collected together in the Tugela Basin and Zululand.

BOTANICAL NAME
Dombeya burgessiae
COMMON NAME
Pink Wild Pear
FAMILY
Malvaceae
NATIVE OF
Tanzania

In 1864 Gerrard moved to Madagascar, where he continued collecting until his death from blackwater fever in 1872. It seems likely that he met Miss Burgess in South Africa which places her as a 19th century woman with an interest in plants, though whether she ever visited South Africa is unclear.

Miss Burgess's plant *Dombeya burgessiae*,[5] was discovered by McKen, grown in the Durban Botanic Garden and named by Gerrard. Interestingly, another woman in this book, Katherine Saunders, was also helped by McKen, who was a Scot, and manager of the Tongaat Estate in South Africa before Katherine's husband took over.[5] Could Miss Burgess have known Katherine Saunders?

In another link, McKen married the sister of John Medley Wood,[4] a South African botanist and fern expert,[6,7] who lived near the mouth of the Umhloti River in South Africa in a house called Otterspool, the same name as the house in Liverpool in which Hannah Moss, also featured in this book, lived. Otterspool is an unusual name – could it be a co-incidence?

There are many references to Miss Burgess in the world of South African botany, but little information about her life.

Mrs R.V. Butt

Hardly any information is available about Mrs Butt. Reports say that in 1910 a crimson *Bougainvillea* was discovered by Mrs Butt in a garden in Cartagena, Colombia[8] while she was visiting from Trinidad.[9] Cuttings were then spread across the Caribbean and subsequently to the rest of the world.

Bougainvillea buttiana was first assumed to be a new species and in 1944 was named by Holttum and Standley.[9] It is now thought to be the first known *Bougainvillea* hybrid between *Bougainvillea glabra* and *Bougainvillea peruviana*. Before this, in the early 20th century, *Bougainvillea buttiana* had been introduced to Europe and from there to Australia and other parts of the world. It also arrived in Florida under another name in 1912-13.

Kew Gardens also distributed plants it had propagated to British colonies.[10] In fact, 'Mrs Butt' is also known as 'Crimson Lake' and 'Scarlet Queen'. Mrs Butt herself was probably a woman with an interest in plants whose first name has not been recorded and is known instead by her husband's initials (or possibly her own?).

BOTANICAL NAME
Bougainvillea buttiana
COMMON NAME
Orange Ice
FAMILY
Nyctaginaceae
NATIVE OF
South America

Mme. Coignet

It is known that Mme. Coignet travelled to Japan with her husband and collected seeds of the Glory Vine in 1875.[11] Mme Coignet lived in Lyon in France and was the daughter of Jean Sisley (1804-1891), a rose enthusiast and expert who was one of the creators of the Lyon Horticultural Circle, later the Lyon Horticultural Association.[12]

BOTANICAL NAME
Vitis coignetiae
COMMON NAME
Crimson Glory Vine
FAMILY
Vitaceae
NATIVE OF
Japan

The first name of Mme. Coignet is not recorded, neither are her dates, though she clearly lived in the 19th century in Lyon. However, the vine was introduced previously by the East India merchants Jardine and Matheson and grown in the nursery of Anthony Waterer at Knapp Hill, Surrey.[11]

The two groups of plants were finally identified and named as *Vitis coignetiae* in 1883. The plant grows vigorously in its native Japan, climbing to the tops of trees and having brilliant red foliage in autumn.

Jeanne Daigremont

French botanists Raymond Hamet and Perrier de la Bathie first described *Kalanchoe daigremontiana* in 1914.

They dedicated the species name to Madame Daigremont, who, with her husband, was a member of the French Society of Botany. Jeanne Daigremont (active 1908-15) was a botanist interested in the culture of alpine plants.[13] Before her marriage she was known as Jeanne Vaucher. *Kalanchoe daigremontiana* is identified in many publications as *Bryophyllum daigremontiana*.

BOTANICAL NAME
Kalanchoe daigremontiana
COMMON NAME
Mother of Thousands,
Mexican Hat Plant
FAMILY
Crassulaceae
NATIVE OF
Madagascar

References

1. *Flora Iberica*. Real Jardin Botanico, Madrid, 2016

2. Clusius, C. *Rariorum plantarum historia*, 1601.

3. Clusius, C. *Rariorum aliquot Stirpium per Hispanias observatarum* Historia, 1576.

4. Gunn, M and Codd, L.E. *Botanical Exploration of Southern Africa: an illustrated history of early botanical literature on Cape flora*. Botanical Research Institute, Cape Town, 1981.

5. *D. burgessiae Gerr*. Ex Harv.& Sond. Flora Capensis 2, 590, 1862. J Bombay Nat. Hist. Soc. 62, 61, 1965.

6. Brown, N. E. *John Medley Wood. 1827-1915*. Bulletin of Miscellaneous Information (Royal Botanic Gardens, Kew) 1915.10 (1915): 417–419.

7. Medley Wood, J. A Handbook to the Flora of Natal. Durban, 1907

8. www.discovercolumbia.com

9. Standley, P.C. & Steyermark, J. *Bougainvillea buttiana Studies of Central American Plants*. In: Publications of the Field Museum of Natural History. Botanical Series 23 (2),44, 1944.

10. *Bougainvillea History*, www.bougainvilleaplant.blogspot.co.uk

11. *Vitis coignetiae* Pulliat ex. Planch. www.beanstreesandshrubs.com.

12. Dickerson, B C. *The Old Rose Advisor*. Volume 1. Choice Press, Lincoln, USA, 2001.

13. Daigremont, J. *Influence de la composition chimique du sol sur la culture des plantes alpines*. Bulletin de la Societe Botanique de France, 59, 469-474, 1912.

CHAPTER
•SEVEN•

Summary

This chapter summarises the characteristics which contributed to the success of the 34 women in this book in having at least one plant named after them.

The features identified here do not all apply to all of the women, but each is important at least to several of them. Of those listed below, the first – wealth – is probably the most significant, with the others presented in no particular order.

Wealth

Many, indeed most, of the women in this book were fortunate in not having to earn a living and so were able to devote much of their time to botanical or horticultural activities.

In the 18th and 19th centuries women of the upper social classes were not expected to work and may have employed women from the lower classes as cooks, nursery maids, and servants, so relieving themselves of the need to take on any household chores. To fill their time, activities such as embroidery, painting – and botanising – were considered suitable occupations for such women. Twelve of the women lived in estates or large houses with substantial gardens where they had the facilities to grow and maintain large numbers of plants, some in stove-houses or greenhouses. In the 18th century six of the twelve women lived in this manner – Charlotte Clive, Maria, Lady Northampton, Diana Beaumont, Emma Tankerville, Hannah Moss and Rosalia von Josika. Five women in the 19th century were in the same position – Louisa Laurence, Mary Barber, Mary Ann Robb, Marianne North and Ellen Willmott. Finally Kathleen Meserve, in the 20th century in the USA, had a large garden in which she cultivated her hollies.

Geography

Being in the right place at the right time was a significant factor in the success of some of the women. Dorothy Hall Berry, Hannah Moss and Elizabeth Harrison lived in or around the city of Liverpool at a time when it was an important trading port with plants being introduced from around the world for identification and propagation.

Women who were born or who emigrated to South Africa found themselves in a country that was largely unexplored and which had a flora of major significance that was ready for introduction to the rest of the world. Such women included Mary Barber, Katherine Saunders, Marianne Mason, Louisa Bolus and Helen Milford. Finally, as outlined in Chapter 5, the US state of Oregon, which is large and has a low population density, provided an excellent location for discovering new and unusual plants by the women who explored there - Almeda Barrett, Nancy Davis and Lilla Leach.

Moving Overseas

Some of the women in this book were able to move away from their country of birth and use the opportunities presented to investigate the flora of countries whose botanical riches were still largely unreported. Family connections were important for some of the women to establish themselves away from their country of birth. Mary Barber emigrated with her family to South Africa at the age of two and developed her interest in the flora of her adopted country as both a collector and artist. Similarly, Katherine Saunders moved to South Africa on her marriage and Marianne Mason to join her brother who was there already. Margaret Mee visited her sister in Brazil and settled there. Mme Coignet travelled to Japan with her husband and Olga Fedchenko travelled to Turkestan after the death of her husband. Three of the women travelled independently; Maria Merian to South America, Mary Ann Robb to Turkey and Marianne North travelled the world.

Family Influences

As well as the influence of family in determining where the women did their botanising, many were from families where other members had interests in botany or horticulture and they were able to use their relatives' knowledge and contacts to further their interests. For Dorothy Berry, Margaret Mee and Mme. Coignet it was their fathers who were the influence in terms of being a botanist, artist and horticulturalist, respectively. Maria Merian was influenced by her step-father who painted pictures of flowers. Elizabeth Harrison's husband was a plant collector, Olga Fedchenko's was a naturalist and Antoinette Danford's was an artist and ornithologist. Matilda Smith's second cousin was Joseph Hooker, Director of Kew, and Louisa Bolus's great-uncle was a botanist. It is perhaps unsurprising that these women followed in the footsteps of their relatives.

Contact with Eminent Botanists and Horticulturalists

As well as these family influences, many of the women featured in this book were in contact with eminent scientists at their local botanic gardens or at Kew to help with plant identification. These women are listed in Table 1.4. A total of eight of the women had links to Kew botanists in various capacities – Mary Barber, Charlotte Clive, Louisa Lawrence, Margaret Mee, Hannah Moss, Marianne North, Mary Ann Robb and Matilda Smith. Other links were with Charles Darwin (Mary Barber), the Dublin Botanic Garden (Mary Barber), John Lindley (Elizabeth Harrison), Asa Gray of the USA (Almeda Barrett), University of Cape Town (Louisa Bolus), St. Petersburg Botanic Garden (Olga Fedchenko) and the Durban Botanic Garden (Miss Burgess and Katherine Saunders).

Ignoring Opposition

In the 18th and 19th centuries women with an interest in plants encountered much opposition, mainly from men, or found that their work was ignored or belittled. Not being allowed to join learned societies also contributed to their being under-rated and ignored. Many discovered the answer was to keep a low profile and not be discouraged. For some, this meant that they were not recognised in their own lifetimes, for example, Maria, Lady Northampton, Dorothy Hall Berry, and Rosalia von Josika. Others were recognised but then became forgotten or obscure such as Emma Tankeville, Diana Beaumont, Anne Marie Libert, Elizabeth Harrison, Hannah Moss and Louisa Lawrence. Some were known in their own country but not elsewhere, including Olga Fedchenko in Russia and Mary Barber, Marianne Harriet Mason and Katherine Saunders in South Africa.

Lack of Formal Training

Many women had no formal training in botany or horticulture but nevertheless were able to become experts in their chosen area. This is not surprising since little formal training of any kind was available to women of the eighteenth and nineteenth centuries. Kathleen Meserve who lived entirely in the twentieth century was proud of having no formal training, while still being able to grow and patent her blue hollies, with considerable success.

Determination and Stamina

The lives of some of the women were characterised by adversity. In the absence of antibiotics and modern medicine it is not unexpected they were affected by illness or the death of a parent, husband or child. The mothers of both Mary Ann Robb and Lilla Leach died shortly after the birth of their children and Almeda Barrett's daughter died and left twins, to be looked after by their grandparents, the Barretts. Mary Ann Robb experienced a further tragedy when her husband died after two years of marriage and Olga Fedchenko's husband was killed after just six years of marriage. Despite these setbacks these women continued to pursue their interests in plants. Some of the women travelled to parts of the world that were undeveloped and had to endure considerable adversity, travel long distances, perhaps on horseback or on foot, at the same time as collecting specimens and returning with them. Was eccentricity the characteristic that spurred some of these women onwards? It was certainly the case for some of them, perhaps coupled with determination and a refusal to give up. For example, Ellen Willmott was certainly eccentric which caused her some difficulties in later life and contributed to her losing her estate after overspending on gardeners and plants.

The women profiled in this book are just a small and eclectic selection of those who could have been included if other sources of information had been accessed. However, it is to be hoped that this volume has gone some way towards highlighting the often unsung contributions these women have made to botanical science. Their contribution will remain forever in those plants named after them.

ACKNOWLEDGEMENTS

There are many people I am pleased to acknowledge for their assistance in the writing of this book. My first thanks go to my parents – another Mary, and Ted. They must have been totally bemused by their only daughter's unexpected interest in plants, but they did not bat an eyelid. I was driven to numerous places near and far to find various plant species to add to my collection of pressed flowers: they let me pursue my interest undisturbed. For that, belated thanks Mum and Dad! Shelagh Todd, director of the horticulture course at Newton Rigg College was supportive when I wanted to do a desk-based project to test my ideas for this book, and for this I am very grateful.

I have used libraries during the course of researching this book. In particular, the wonderful library of the Lakeland Horticultural Society at Holehird Gardens, Windermere has been an excellent source of material and I am privileged to be a member of the Society. I also consulted the Royal Horticultural Society's Lindley Library in London and found the staff there to be unfailingly helpful. Thanks specifically to Tom Pink, Lucy Waitt and Susan Robin. Craig Brough, Lynn Parker and Joanna Evans of the Royal Botanic Gardens Library, Kew also helped with information and I am grateful for that too.

I discovered the book 'John Moss' by Graham Trust whilst trying to find the first name of Mrs Moss and wrote to him to see if he could help. He very kindly, as he put it "nipped down to the churchyard where the Moss clan are buried" and came back with two possible names. We eventually agreed that the dates indicated that Mrs Moss's name was Hannah. Thank you Graham – I enjoyed your book too!

Special help with sourcing pictures and additional information was provided by the following people who went to extra lengths to assist (in alphabetical order): Marcus Bicknell, Hilary Birks, Tony and Marion Morrison, Gary A. Monroe, David Porter and Paul Tanner-Tremaine - very many thanks. Other sources of information were provided by Lord Allendale, Anne-Lise Fourie, Beverly Galloway, Shawna Gandy, Emilie Hardman, Mary-Sue Ittner, David Leverton, Darryl Lundy, Steve Matson, Holly Parkin, Tracy Robillard, Sian Phillips, Sandra Turck and Rebecca Woolfrey – thank you all.

This book would not have been possible without Russell Holden of Pixel Tweaks, my book producer. His help and attention to detail is what has made this book a reality. Thanks, Russ. Proof reading has been the task of my husband Henry, something he is very good at, having had lots of experience and I thank him very much. I must, however, emphasise that any as yet undiscovered errors or omissions remain mine alone. The book has been greatly enhanced by the wonderful paintings by Sophie Holme on the front cover and for the chapter headings. Sophie has an unerring capacity to get her drawings and paintings exactly right for their context. Very many thanks for all of them.

In reality I have written this book for my family, so, in addition to my granddaughter Mary, to whom this book is dedicated, Henry, David and Sarah, and Matt and Louise, this is for you! I hope you enjoy reading it.

Brenda Leese October 2017.

•APPENDIX•

List of Plants

Beaumontia grandiflora Wall.
Biphrenaria harrisoniae (Hooker) Rchb.f.
Bolusanthemum tugwelliae (l.Bolus) Schwantes.
Bougainvillea buttiana Holttum & Standl.
Brassia lawrenceana Lindl.
Brimeura amethystina Salisb.
Cattleya mossiae C.Parker ex Hook.
Ceratostigma willmottianum Stapf.
Clivia miniata (Lindl.) Verschaff.
Crocosmia masonorum (L.Bolus) N.E.Br.
Diascia barberae Hook.f.
Dombeya burgessiae Gerr. ex Harv.& Sond.
Euphorbia robbiae Turrill.
Fittonia albivenis (Lindl. ex Veitch) Brummitt.
Haemanthus katherinae Bak.
Hardenbergia comptoniana (Andrews) Benth.
Helichrysum milfordii. Killick.
Ilex x meserveae. S.Y. Hu
Ipomoea horsfalliae Hook.
Iris danfordiae Baker.
Kalanchoe daigrementiana Raym.-Hamet & H.Perrier.
Kalmiopsis leachiana (L.F.Hend,) Rehder.
Kniphofia northiae Baker.
Leucothoe davisiae Torr. ex. A.Gray.
Libertia grandiflora (R.Br.) Sweet.
Neoregelia margaretae L.B.Smith.
Ornithogalum saundersiae Baker.
Penstemon barrrettiae A.Gray
Phaius tankervilleae (Banks & L'Herit.) Bl.
Rosa fedtschenkoana Regel.
Smithiantha cinnabarina (Linden) Kuntze
Syringa josikaea J.Jacq. ex Rchb.f.
Vitis coignetiae Pulliat ex Planch.
Watsonia meriana (L.) Mill.

Note: The plants may have alternative names or have been renamed.

Picture Credits

The author would like to thank the copyright holders for granting permission to reproduce the images illustrated. Every attempt has been made to trace accurate ownership of copyrighted images in this book. Any errors or omissions will be corrected in subsequent editions provided notification is sent to the publisher.

Chapter 1

Linnaeus Garden: B.Leese; The SS Great Western, 1882: WikiCommons/public domain; Wardian Case: WikiCommons,/public domain.

Chapter 2

Maria Sibylla Merian: 1679: public domain; *Watsonia meriana* : Mary Sue Ittner: PBS Wiki; Emma Tankerville: Private Collection Photo@Philip Mould Ltd, London/Bridgeman Images; *Phaius tankervilliae*: Pierre-Joseph Redoute/ WikiCommons/public domain; *Phaius tankervilliae:* Barbosella: WikiCommons CC-BY-SA-2.0; Diana Beaumont: Lord Allendale; *Beaumontia grandiflora*: Shu Suehiro: WikiCommons GNU-CC-3.0; Maria Northampton: painted by Eliza Chute; *Hardenbergia comptoniana*: Michael Wolf: WikiCommons CC-SA-3.0; Anne-Marie Libert: Cercle Royal Marie-Anne Libert de Malmedy, (Belgique); *Libertia grandiflora*: Velela: WikiCommons/public domain; *Ipomoea horsfalliae*: Kurt Stuber: WikiCommons CC-BY-SA 3.0; Charlotte Clive: T.A.Dean La Belle Ensemble 1829; *Cliva miniata*: B. Leese; *Cattleya mossiae* drawing: Walter Hood Fitch: Curtis's Botanical Magazine vol. 65, 1839: WikiCommons/public domain; *Cattleya mossiae*: Danniegugu: WikiCommons CC-BY-SA 3.0; *Biphrenaria harrisoniae:* Dalton Holland Baptista: WikiCommons CC-SA-3.0 GNU; *Fittonia albivenis* 'Verschaffeltii' B.Leese; Pages from 'Conversations on Botany': Fitton, E. Conversations on Botany. Longman, Rees, Orme, Brown and Green, London, 7th edition, 1817: public domain; *Syringa josikaea*: Sten Porse license CC-BY-SA-3.0: WikiCommons.

Chapter 3

Louisa Lawrence: Chipgc: WikiCommons CC-BY-SA 3.0; *Brassia lawrenciana*: Miss Drake (1803-1857) del., G.Barclay sc. – Edwards Bot Register 2 (N.s.4) plate 18. public domain; Mary Barber: Paul Tanner-Tremaine: www.1820settlers.com; *Diasca barberae*: El Grafo: WikiCommons CC-BY-SA 3.0; Katherine Saunders: CC-PD-Mark WikiCommons/public domain; Blood Lily: Curtis's Botanical Mag 1884; *Haemanthus katherinae:* Do Tuan Hung: WikiCommons; CC-BY-SA 3.0; *Ornithogalum saundersiae*: Noricus 1969: WikiCommons

PD; Mary Ann Robb: J Roy Hort Soc 98, facing p.307, 1973. *Euphorbia robbiae*: Frank Vincatz: WikiCommons CC-BY-SA 3.0; Marianne North: WikiCommons/ public domain; *Kniphofia northiae*: peganum: WikiCommons CC-BY-SA; Olga Fedchenko: WikiCommons/ public domain; *Rosa fedtschenkoana*: Nadiatalent: WikiCommons CC-SA 4.0; Marianne Harriet Mason: The Board of Trustees of the Royal Botanic Gardens, Kew; *Crocosmia masonorum*: peganum: WikiCommons CC-BY-SA; Small Alpine Nerine: J Roy Hort Soc 39, facing p.8, 1913; *Iris danfordiae*: Ghislain118: WikiCommons CC-BY-SA; Matilda Smith: out of copyright; *Smithiantha cinnabarina*: Magnus Manske: WikiCommons CC-SA 2.0; Ellen Willmott: info@clarencebicknell.com; *Ceratostigma willmottianum* Wouter Hagens: WikiCommons CC-BY-SA 3.0; Warley Place: info@clarencebicknell.com; Louisa Bolus: In: Glen, H.F & Germishuizen, G. (compilers) 2010. Botanical Exploration of Southern Africa. Edition 2. Strelitzia 26, South African National Biodiversity Institute (SANBI), Pretoria, South Africa, page 101; *Bolusanthemum tugwelliae*: Bolusanthemum wiki: Scot.zona CC-BY-3-2.0; *Helicrysum milfordii*: Hilary Birks.

Chapter 4

Kathleen Meserve: Barton Silverman/The New York Times/Redux/eyevine; *Ilex x meserviae*: B Leese; Margaret Mee: Tony Morrison; *Neoregelia rosea:* RBG Kew/Marcello Sellaro; *Sobralia margaretae:* Guido Pabst/Tony Morrison.

Chapter 5

Mount Hood: B Leese; Oregon countryside: B Leese; Lilla Leach's house: B Leese; Johnson Creek: B Leese; *Kalmiopsis leachiana:* B Leese; *Penstemon barrettiae:* Gary A Monroe hosted by the USDA-NRCS PLANTS database; *Leucothoe davisiae*: Steve Matson; Nancy Jane Davis: Grier School; *Kalmiopsis leachiana* flower: Diana Karabut; Lilla and John Leach: Oregon Historical Society: Negative Number OrHi66620, John and Lilla Leach Collection, Org. Lot370, Box 3, Folder39.

Chapter 6

Brimeura amethystina: Meneerke Bloem: WikiCommons: CC-BY-SA 3.0; *Dombeya burgessiae*: Consultaplantas: WikiCommons CC-BY-SA 3.0; *Bougainvillea buttiana:*: Hectonichus: WikiCommons CC-SA-3.0; *Vitis coignetiae* : Sten Porse: WikiCommons license CC-SA-3.0GNU; *Kalanchoe diagremontiana*: Marcelle7: WikiCommons CC-SA 3.0.

Chapter 7

Potting shed & plant pots photographs courtesy of Russell Holden.

INDEX

Lightning Source UK Ltd.
Milton Keynes UK
UKRC01n1018120318
319148UK00001B/8